Praise for *The Radical Promise*

"*The Radical Promise* is a masterclass in the magnetism and magic of integrity. Farber, Kouzes, and Posner deliver a soul-stirring "parable-plus" that transforms accountability from a weary duty into a radical competitive advantage. It is a brilliant, heart-centered compass for any leader eager to turn hollow talk into a solid walk."

—Chip R. Bell
author of *Inside Your Customer's Imagination*

"Anyone interested in becoming an even better leader of character needs to grab a copy of *The Radical Promise* right now. The authors, legends in the field of leadership, have written best-selling books that deliver acclaimed models and principles used in classrooms and boardrooms around the world. In this new work, they pack that world-class content into a concise, fun, and practical volume. The conversational tone makes for easy reading and internalizing of the leadership lessons. Shelves are filled with good books on leadership, but I "promise" you this is one you'll enjoy reading and won't want to put down. *The Radical Promise* is unique because it imparts extolled leadership principles through a captivating workplace parable. Rather than prescribing how to lead, the authors invite readers on a journey of self-discovery to learn that leadership is a relationship that begins with integrity and is built on trust, values, and relationships. Don't miss this opportunity to take your leadership to the next level; *The Radical Promise* will help you learn how to become the leader people follow because they *want* to, not because they *must*."

—Sandra Stosz

Vice Admiral US Coast Guard (ret.), former Superintendent of the US Coast Guard Academy and author of *Breaking Ice and Breaking Glass: Leading in Uncharted Waters*

"I have long admired the exceptional work of Jim Kouzes and Barry Posner on credibility and leadership, and *The Radical Promise* extends that legacy in a highly compelling and engaging way. Partnering with the insightful Steve Farber, they bring to life the essential truth that doing what you say you will do is not just good practice; it is the very foundation of effective leadership. It is a powerful and timely reminder that trust is built in the simple yet profound act of making and keeping commitments."

—Stephen M. R. Covey

The New York Times and #1 *Wall Street Journal* bestselling author of *The Speed of Trust* and *Trust & Inspire*

"The leadership conversation is often full of complexity, but the truth about credibility is surprisingly straightforward: keep your promises. In *The Radical Promise*, Farber, Kouzes, and Posner bring that truth to life in a way that is both challenging and deeply practical. This book asks leaders to drop the stories, the blame, and the excuses—and focus on the only thing that actually builds trust: consistent follow-through. That's why this message matters right now.

It applies across industries, across roles, and across cultures. When leaders internalize this idea, everything changes."

—Cy Wakeman

The New York Times bestselling author, *No Ego,*
and *Reality-Based Leadership*

"I truly believe most of us at least *try* to do what we say we will do. But holding ourselves accountable can be a complex goal to achieve. Steve Farber, Jim Kouzes, and Barry Posner show us how to achieve this hidden desire through a fun parable we can all relate to. Read *The Radical Promise* and learn how to be true to yourself—and everyone else!"

—Ken Blanchard

coauthor of *The One Minute Manager®*
and *Simple Truths of Leadership*

"Based on decades of real-life experience with leaders, the authors spin a story about the ups and downs of leadership. Not just entertaining, it is also informative about how people win and lose credibility and how they rebuild it. There are lessons here for everyone, regardless of your position. With real-life plot twists, it could very well be a Netflix streaming series."

—Nilofer Merchant

Co-Founder of Intangible Labs & author of *Our Best Work.*

"Leadership is simple, but not easy. At its core, leadership comes down to one thing: do what you say you will do. When words and actions align, trust grows. When they do not, culture erodes. The Radical Promise is a powerful reminder that credibility is not a slogan. It is a daily discipline. Through a compelling story grounded in decades of research, Steve Farber, Jim Kouzes, and Barry Posner show us what happens when leaders forget that business is personal, and how to rebuild when we fall short. This book reinforces a truth I have learned over a lifetime of leading: values are real only when they are lived. Culture is not created by posters on the wall. It is created by promises kept. If you want to build a workplace where people feel safe, valued, and inspired to give their best, start here. This is a book about integrity, courage, and the radical act of being accountable to your own words."

—Garry Ridge

Chairman Emeritus, WD-40 Company,
USA Today bestselling author, *Any Dumb Ass Can Do It*

"*The Radical Promise* is a timely and deeply resonant reminder that the health of any culture—team, organization, or community—rests on trust. And trust, as Steve Farber so powerfully brings to life alongside Jim Kouzes and Barry Posner, is built in the smallest, most human of moments: when we do what we say we will do.

What makes this book so compelling is its ability to translate a foundational leadership truth into a lived experience. Through story, it reveals how credibility is not an abstract concept, but a daily practice—one that shapes connection, strengthens accountability, and ultimately determines whether people feel safe, seen, and willing to bring their best.

In a time when so many workplaces are struggling with disengagement and disconnection, *The Radical Promise* offers something both simple and profound: a path back to alignment between words and actions. For leaders committed to restoring trust, cultivating meaningful relationships, and building cultures where people and performance can truly thrive, this book is essential reading."

—Adam Markel

Co-Founder, WORKWELL Labs;
Wall Street Journal bestselling author of
Pivot, Change Proof and *Re-Culture*

"In *The Radical Promise*, Farber, Kouzes, and Posner get to the heart of it: credibility is built—or broken—in the gap between what we say and what we do. So, do what you say you will do (DWYSYWD). Every time. This isn't soft leadership. It's disciplined, love-based leadership—with love as the standard and accountability as the practice. The story had me laughing out loud and, at times, moved to tears. It has stayed with me and challenged me to reflect on and sharpen what I believe."

—Ilana Wisby

Quantum & Deep Tech Entrepreneur,
Founding CEO, Oxford Quantum Circuits Limited

"Jim Kouzes and Barry Posner are legends in the world of leadership development. Now joined by author Steve Farber, they have turned their lessons into stories. *The Radical Promise: Mastering the Art of Doing What You Say You Will Do* offers the insights you have come to expect, paired with the artistry of master storytellers. The result is an engaging guide that anyone new to management—or well settled into a leadership role—will want on their bookshelf."

—John Baldoni

award-winning author of more than a dozen leadership books and three collections of poetry, including his newest, *Leadership in Verse*

"Leadership ultimately rises or falls on trust—and trust depends on whether you do what you say you will do. In *The Radical Promise*, Steve Farber, Jim Kouzes, and Barry Posner blend masterful storytelling with decades of leadership wisdom to issue a simple yet demanding challenge: hold yourself 100% accountable to your words. This book is a timely reminder that credibility, culture, and trust are forged through disciplined follow-through. *The Radical Promise* is a compelling and practical call to radical accountability for anyone who aspires to lead with integrity."

—Tom Collins

Professor of Pediatrics and author of the award-winning book, *The Four Stars of Leadership*

"*The Radical Promise* captures what I've always believed sits at the heart of meaningful business relationships: trust is earned through consistent follow-through. At BNI, we believe that "Givers Gain," and that principle only works when people do what they say they will do—every time. Farber, Kouzes, and Posner have created an entertaining, provocative and compelling story that reinforces the discipline of trust, reliability, accountability. This book is a powerful guide to becoming the kind of professional and leader others are eager to engage with."

—Ivan Misner, Ph.D.
Founder, BNI

"*The Radical Promise*, co-authored by leadership luminaries Steve Farber, Jim Kouzes, and Barry Posner, is a business allegory that truly packs a punch. Having read the authors' previous works, I had high expectations. This book not only met them—it exceeded them. Written in an engaging, highly accessible style, it delivers powerful insights and practical wisdom—I found myself pulling out pure gems throughout."

—David M. Corbin
five-time *Wall Street Journal* Bestselling Author of *Illuminate* and *Preventing BrandSlaughter*

"At a time when trust in leaders has never been lower, *The Radical Promise* cuts straight to the heart of what rebuilds it. Through a story that pulls you in and won't let go, Kouzes, Posner, and Farber illuminate the one practice that underpins everything in leadership: keeping your word. If you want to be a leader worthy of following, this book belongs in your hands."

—Dr. Margie Warrell
leadership speaker, advisor &
bestselling author of *The Courage Gap*

"This book got under my skin, in a good way. Farber, Kouzes, and Posner turn credibility into concrete action: the small commitments that earn trust every day and what it takes to rebuild it once it's lost. The twist I didn't expect, and loved, is that Jim and Barry step into the narrative as coaches, which makes the whole book feel lived-in, not lectured. Wise, practical, and genuinely transformative, this one stays with you."

—Adrian Gostick

The New York Times bestselling author of

Leading with Gratitude and *All In*

"In a world where promises are made casually and commitments are treated as flexible, *The Radical Promise* restores gravity to our words. Farber, Kouzes, and Posner remind us that credibility is not built through charisma or authority but through the disciplined alignment of what we say and what we do. Through the journeys of Janice, Cat, Simon, and a compelling ensemble of characters, the authors bring decades of credibility research to life in ways that are both practical and deeply human. This book does more than explain why credibility matters; it challenges each of us to raise our personal standard and to live up to the promises we make. It is a timely call to integrity in an era that too often normalizes its absence."

—Leo Bottary

Author of *Peernovation*

"*Do what you say you will do.* Sounds like a simple tenet, but for leaders the notion can be a slippery slope. Through a compelling story and prescriptive actions, *The Radical Promise* provides a path to personal and organizational success. Faber, Kouzes, and Posner are all leadership experts who provide a human approach to leadership that these times require. Just when you thought there was nothing new to be learned about leadership, the authors show us that promises kept are what really matter in leadership."

—Richard A. Moran

former CEO and college president, author of *The Accidental Vineyard* and *Never Say Whatever*

"This gripping parable pulls you in, with sharp plot twists and a story every leader should hear. Beneath the narrative lies a powerful message: leadership lives or dies in the commitments we make and the trust we build. It's also a cautionary tale about what happens when leaders neglect culture and values. Leaders, let this radical promise burrow into your bones and seep into your soul. Your team, organization, and legacy depend on it."

—Gregg Vanourek

TEDx speaker and award-winning co-author, *LIFE Entrepreneurs* and *Triple Crown Leadership*

"Steve Farber's *The Radical Leap* has been one of the few leadership books I've routinely handed to agency owners for years, because it captures something most business books miss: leadership should be unapologetically personal, rooted in love, and relentlessly oriented toward action. In *The Radical Promise*, Steve—joined by Jim Kouzes and Barry Posner—has taken that original parable and raised the stakes. This story forces you to wrestle with the hard, uncomfortable side of leadership: your credibility, your follow-through, and the gap between what you say and what you actually do. I see that gap every day in agencies around the world, and I can tell you this: the idea of making a "radical promise" to Do What You Say You Will Do is both brutally simple and profoundly transformative. The narrative makes that principle tangible and memorable in a way no checklist or framework ever could. If you lead a company, a team, or a client relationship, this book is required reading. It will challenge you, call you out, and then equip you to rebuild trust with your people by aligning your words, your values, and your behavior in the moments that matter most."

—Drew McLellan
CEO, Agency Management Institute

"Great leadership begins with a simple, radical act: doing what you say you will do. *The Radical Promise* connects that truth to something in all the great leaders I work with—that your superpowers only shine when people can trust you to show up as the real you, every time. Farber, Kouzes, and Posner have written a book that doesn't just inspire. It holds you accountable."

—Sanyin Siang
CEO Advisor and Duke University Professor

"Most people read a book because of the title. Read this book because of the subtitle. My mentor Steve Farber and his friends Jim Kouzes and Barry Posner have been mastering the art of doing what you say you will do for years. And now they are teaching the rest of us how to lead and love others by our actions and not just our words."

—Tommy Spaulding
The New York Times bestselling author of
The Heart-Led Leader and *The Gift of Influence*

"In *The Radical Promise*, Steve Farber, Jim Kouzes, and Barry Posner remind us of a principle that is both simple and profound: credibility is earned by doing what you say you will do. In an environment where trust is the foundation of every relationship with employees, partners, and customers, this idea is not just relevant; it is essential. It is easy to focus on major milestones, but it is the daily actions, the meetings we show up prepared for, the deadlines we honor, and the conversations we follow through on that ultimately define our leadership and shape our culture.

The Radical Promise is a timely reminder that leadership is not about intention; it is about integrity in action. I encourage you to reflect on your own commitments and consider the impact of consistently delivering on them. Because in the end, trust is not granted; it is earned, one promise at a time."

—Hector Fernandez
CEO, IGT

"Steve Farber, along with his mentors Jim Kouzes and Barry Posner, has done it again with an entertaining story and a powerful reminder that leading with love and genuine care for others isn't just the right thing to do, it's the foundation for building an extraordinary culture and achieving meaningful financial success. I know from my experience at Trailer Bridge, when you pour into people, everything else follows. And when it comes to living out your DWYSYWD, the magic really happens when you do it alongside the people who matter most—friends, family, and a team that lifts each other higher. That's how you create something special. . .and absolutely crush it."

—Mitch Luciano
CEO, Trailer Bridge

"*The Radical Promise* gets straight to the point: leaders who keep their word inspire trust, loyalty, and results. In any business—just like in my business of rock and roll—that's what separates the real pros from the pretenders. While the phrase "take it to the next level" can sound overwrought, that is exactly what Farber, Kouzes and Posner have done. This book is truly "next level" advice about how the foundation of trust & leadership leads in a straight line to SUCCESS!"

—Jay Jay French

Founder, Manager, Guitarist, Twisted Sister; co-author, Twisted Business: Lessons from My Life in Rock 'n' Roll

"I read *The Radical Leap* in 2008, and it helped shape the vision for EVOTEK before we ever opened our doors. Steve Farber's philosophy of conscious capitalism and Extreme Leadership became foundational to how we built our culture. In *The Radical Promise*, Steve and his longtime mentors and leadership legends, Jim Kouzes and Barry Posner, raise the bar even higher. This book challenges leaders to live up to who they say they are. It's bold, honest, and deeply necessary."

—Cesar Enciso

Founder and CEO, EVOTEK

THE RADICAL PROMISE

STEVE FARBER | JAMES M. KOUZES | BARRY Z. POSNER

THE RADICAL PROMISE

MASTERING THE ART OF DOING WHAT YOU SAY *You Will Do*

WILEY

Published by John Wiley & Sons, Inc., Hoboken, New Jersey.

For general information on our other products and services or for technical support, please contact our Customer Care Department within the United States at (800) 762-2974, outside the United States at (317) 572-3993 or fax (317) 572-4002.

Wiley also publishes its books in a variety of electronic formats. Some content that appears in print may not be available in electronic formats. For more information about Wiley products, visit our web site at www.wiley.com.

Library of Congress Cataloging-in-Publication Data is Available:

ISBN 9781394426966 (Cloth)
ISBN 9781394426973 (ePub)
ISBN 9781394426980 (ePDF)

Cover Design: Wiley
Cover Images: sgtphoto/Getty Images, komkrit Preechachanwate/Shutterstock
Author Photos: Paul Andrew, Scott McCue Photography, Courtesy of the Authors

Printed and bound by CPI Group (UK) Ltd, Croydon CR0 4YY
C9781394426966_020726

Contents

Preface *xix*

The Radical Promise *1–192*

Putting Promise into Practice: A Field Guide for Action *193*

For Further Reading *229*

Acknowledgments *235*

About the Authors *239*

Preface

What you are about to read is often referred to as a business "parable"—a fictional story that conveys a lesson. So, yes, this story is a work of fiction, but you can rest assured that it's based on very real characters and circumstances. What's most important, however, is that the lessons and ideas that you're about to experience are anything but fictional. They are rooted in a great deal of research that's been going on for decades, and they will serve you well, should you commit to putting them into practice.

As for the narrative, consider it a cautionary tale of sorts. Now, that may sound dire or ominous, but I think you'll find that most of all, it's a story of hope and promise, challenge and opportunity. First, we need to establish a little context and make a few important introductions.

My name is Steve Farber—just "Farber" to my friends—and I'll be your narrator, your guide, in this experience. In my career of more than three decades as a leadership consultant, coach, author, and speaker, I've had the opportunity to work with literally every kind of industry and company you can imagine. And "literally" is a word I use literally.

I've worked with many of these organizations in the public and private, for-profit and nonprofit, government and education sectors to build cultures of leadership. So I've been deeply involved with the study of leadership and the practice of leadership. I've been writing about it (my first book, *The Radical Leap: A Personal Lesson in Extreme Leadership*, came out way back in 2004), speaking about it, and advising leaders from across the organizational landscape for over thirty years.

And I'm the first to admit that I don't have it all figured out. I'm not the Answer Man, and I'm certainly not a human Magic 8 Ball. As much as I've learned from my mentors, colleagues, and clients, I miss things from time to time. Or I get stuck. And at times like those, as in the scenario you're about to discover, I find myself going back to my roots, to my knowledge source, to the people who set me on my professional trajectory in the first place: world-renowned leadership gurus Jim Kouzes and Barry Posner.

Jim and Barry are the co-authors of *The Leadership Challenge* and *Credibility* (among other leadership books), and their working relationship, which started in 1982, has produced the most significant body of research on effective leadership on the planet. And I do mean *planet*. Their work has been studied and validated on every continent on Earth. So, you know . . . they're the proverbial GOATs on the subject. And I can't tell you what an honor it is for me to have coauthored this book with these legends.

Here's how Jim, Barry, and I first connected.

In the early days of my career, Barry was the dean of the Business school at Santa Clara University, and Jim was the president of the Tom Peters Company. In 1994, Jim hired me to be on the facilitator team primarily responsible for delivering workshops on his and Barry's work. I was in my thirties then, and starry-eyed to be in the presence of luminaries like him and Barry and, of course, the company's founder, Tom Peters, who was the management guru's management guru.

I had been with the company for about a year, when one day Jim asked me to take a walk with him in the Palo Alto, California, neighborhood where we were based.

"We would like you to join the executive team as vice president and focus your attention on hiring and training other consultant-facilitators," he said.

I was floored.

"We want you to find and develop more people like you," he said in his characteristically gracious and humble style. It was one of the most profound experiences of acknowledgment and confirmation I'd ever had. It still is.

At the time, I was thirty-seven years old and most of our senior executive clients were older and more seasoned than I was. So I always knew that I had to prove my worth and my credibility, that I had to earn my place at the table in every workshop and engagement—especially since I'd never held a senior-level leadership position myself. Now Jim was recognizing my value, not by a pat on the back, but by giving me the opportunity to step up and expand my own leadership experience and capabilities.

Over time, with my mentors' and colleagues' unwavering support, I developed my own point of view, left the Tom Peters Company, and set out on my own to try and make my unique contribution to the world of business and its leaders through a body of work I call Extreme Leadership. Jim and Barry encouraged me every step of my journey, and we would talk occasionally and check in from time to time. But I was out there on my own, doing my thing with clients and—for the most part—having a great time along the way.

My new path led me to the writing of *The Radical Leap*, in which I told the story of a fictional company called XinoniX (pronounced Zi-non-ix), and created the character of Janice Everson, one of the company's young executives—and it's her continuing leadership journey that you're about to witness herein.

But before you dive into the story, I ask you to consider this: Have you ever had that moment when you look at yourself in the mirror and ask yourself if you're being 100% true to yourself? If you're being the best possible leader, or friend, or spouse or, well, person you could possibly be? Those are the questions Janice will have to ask of herself. And in our writing about the quest to help Janice through her troubled times, I took a good, hard look in the mirror, too. And, for me, sometimes the answer to those questions was a resounding *no*.

Our hope is that this story will serve as a mirror of sorts for you. You may not always like what you see squinting back at you (I know I didn't), but that's okay. None of us is perfect. The technical term for that is "being human."

The good news is that we're all in this together, and we can help one another to live up to the promise of a deeply fulfilling life at work and beyond.

And that's a radical promise, indeed.

CHAPTER 1

Unbeknownst to her, Janice Everson was heading for the chopping block.

She was driving her dark blue Audi up the freeway from Mission Beach to Sorrento Valley on an overcast summer day in San Diego County, California.

We call it "June Gloom" around here, and San Diegans don't like it very much. We take any cloud in the sky as a personal affront, so days on end of a perpetual marine layer feels like an all-out onslaught on our sensibilities.

Today, though, the cloud cover over the ocean was nothing compared to the pall spreading over Janice's internal landscape.

Everything had gone so well in the years since she took over as CEO of the small biotech company XinoniX. What she and her team had accomplished was nothing short of astounding. Teddy Garrison, the founder and leader, had suddenly bailed out, and Janice and her team were forced to pick up the pieces in a hurry.

They did far more than that.

I'd known Janice for years at that point, and I always loved her passion for people and her tenacity in the face of obstacles. As both her coach and her friend, I saw up close that she was quick-witted, savvy, and intelligent, but she also had a deep heart for, and belief in, the people she worked with—and she wasn't afraid to show it.

So I wasn't in the least bit surprised when Janice eventually rose to the permanent CEO position of XinoniX. She took up the torch of Teddy's legacy and revitalized the culture around his founding principles, which he called The Radical LEAP: Love, Energy, Audacity, and Proof. They incorporated the principles into their performance appraisals, interview processes, management training, and rewards programs. They held each other accountable for living up to the ideals every day—even etching the words into the walls and windows of the corporate office as a permanent reminder of what they stood for. They galvanized their associates by creating a culture that at every level cultivated Love for the business and each other, generated the Energy and enthusiasm required to overcome any obstacle, inspired an Audacious all-possibilities mindset in their quest to change the world for the better, and provided Proof of their success by producing bottom-line results and by living up to their values, promises, and commitments. They went on to win awards from their peers in the industry, earn the admiration of the San Diego community, and secure spots as a best place to work both in the county of San Diego and in the mid-sized biotech category nationally. And their customers loved them, too. A foray into the world of personal health tech garnered them a net promoter score that was the envy of the industry, and a rapid growth spurt landed them on the Inc 500 as the thirtieth fastest-growing company in the United States.

XinoniX's functioning as a well-oiled machine gave Janice the confidence to pursue her extracurricular pet project of bringing a program to high school students, equipping them with the tools to discover their purpose while they're still young and, through that, help them to find success in their adult lives. She was well aware—painfully at times—that she lived a life of great privilege. Yes, she'd earned it; no one had served up her station on a silver platter, but she saw that kids today seemed to be struggling more with finding themselves than her generation had. She desperately wanted to do her part in helping them find their way as she had done. It was a noble endeavor that gave her a lot of energy, and it served the additional benefit of launching XinoniX into the limelight as a shining example of corporate social responsibility. To give herself more time to focus on her passion project, Janice had personally recruited and added to the team an experienced, top-tier executive as the chief operating officer (COO) to run the increasingly complex day-to-day operations of the business.

In other words, Janice and her team had rocked it, bigtime.

I'm not saying it was because of the coaching work I'd done with her. And I'm not implying with false modesty that it really was that by saying that it *wasn't*. But because of my close relationship with Janice, I was privileged to have seen the XinoniX cultural transformation up close.

But now, for reasons that seem obvious in retrospect, everything was—what's the technical term for it?—going to shit.

And, for the record, I'm not saying that was because of my coaching, either.

The pandemic had blown the people of XinoniX apart—just like it had done to nearly every other business on the planet. In the aftermath of the living-in-Zoom times, Janice and her executive team had coaxed folks to return to the office for at least three days a week. And, at first, things just felt different. The laughter in the hallways was gone. Almost all had eschewed the by-then-optional mask wearing, and even though she found it lovely to see everyone's faces again, Janice noticed that the newly revealed expressions were more grim than glad. And instead of hanging out together and grabbing a drink after work, most people jetted off for home at the end of the workday. Or before.

Love? Energy? Not so much.

But little by little, the pre-pandemic work environment had returned, and most folks were in the office most days. The interpersonal dynamics were on the mend and people's physical and mental health had recovered well, but another kind of virus—a malaise of doubt, discouragement, and a feeling of being undervalued—had taken hold in the still-recovering culture. And this one was being spread by a particular individual—and someone she had personally recruited to be on her own executive team, no less.

We still have some serious culture repair work to do, and I'm going to have to make some big changes at the top, she thought as she parked her car in the company lot and headed to the conference room where the board meeting was about to begin.

Filled with a vague sense of foreboding, Janice pulled open the heavy glass door and stepped inside.

She was right; there was a lot to be done. But she wouldn't get the chance to do it.

Because she'd had an ominous feeling about this meeting, Janice had asked me to accompany her, and I stepped into the conference room just moments after she'd arrived.

I'm sure I'm no different than most folks, but from the moment I walk into a room, I can feel the energy—the vibe. And this place felt as cold and thick as motor oil in the icebox.

I saw Janice being greeted by Alastair Langstrom, the current COO she'd personally recruited, and five members of the board. Maybe "greeted" is too generous a word, because when I looked around the room, they were anything but welcoming. Half smiles at best. A little bit of nervous laughter around the table. Langstrom shot me a quick, expressionless glance as he walked over to Janice, hand extended. She took it, gave him a quick, cursory shake, and took her seat at the head of the table. Langstrom walked stiffly to the other end directly across from her, sat down, and motioned to everyone else to do the same. Which they did, in an increasingly awkward silence. I took a seat in the back.

I noticed, with a growing sense of unease, that the board members all had their eyes on Alley—not on Janice.

"Janice," Langstrom said calmly. "The board is in agreement that the time has come for you and XinoniX to part ways."

Son of a bitch, I thought, referring more to the situation than the speaker. *I really should have seen that coming*. And right then, that little time machine in my brain whisked me back through all the events leading up to this moment, starting with nearly one year earlier and the first time I'd met the now-infamous Alastair Langstrom.

CHAPTER 2

My default mode has always been to like people, so it's no surprise that I liked Alastair Langstrom immediately. I recognized him from his pictures in the various articles I'd read, as well as the image on his LinkedIn profile. He stood politely as I approached his table in the famed Chat Bar and Grill in Menlo Park, California.

I always enjoyed my visits to Silicon Valley. I had spent several of my formative years working at the Tom Peters Company office in Palo Alto a couple of miles from this very establishment. Even though the Bay Area was a short flight up the coast from San Diego, it had eluded me in recent years. In fact, I couldn't think of the last time I'd visited. The world had changed significantly since the mid-1990s when I'd worked there, but the vibe of the Valley hadn't really changed at all. The energy in the air, the palpable feeling of emerging and undiscovered possibility, and the collection of young, diverse, ridiculously talented people engaged in a vibrant buzz of conversation made me feel a little nostalgic for my own youthful years in that neighborhood.

I was happy that Janice had asked me to make the trip to check out her top candidate for the position of XinoniX COO, and, of course, through extensive online sleuthing, I'd already learned a good deal about him.

Alastair Langstrom had always wanted to be a CEO. He wanted to make his mark on the world before he turned forty, and he was one of the few in his age group, he believed, who actually gave a rip about the legacy he would leave after he was gone from this planet. From the time he was a student in high school, he'd intended one day to be remembered as the chief executive others counted on to create big, profitable companies valued by analysts and shareholders alike. And, for him, to paraphrase the old saying, failure in that pursuit was not an option.

Alastair, or Alley, as his friends called him, grew up in the Boston area, got his BS in management and leadership from Boston College, headed west to get his MBA at Stanford, and was recruited posthaste by one of the countless tech start-ups popping up like so many bubbles in the Silicon Valley region. But he didn't stay there, or anywhere, for very long. He bounced from company to company, perching for a couple of years on a few different org charts as he steadily and surely made a name for himself and built a reputation as a multifunctional, high-level executive who could streamline operations and drive revenue. He'd worn the titles of chief revenue officer and chief operations officer and even had one short and mildly successful stint as chief marketing officer. He'd had gigs in AI, medical devices, and biotech companies, which gave him a broad view of the cutting-edge business landscape. As his notoriety grew, colleagues and competitors started calling him "Valley Alley," and he wore the nickname proudly like a badge of honor.

Valley Alley had become a bona fide Silicon Valley C-suite player, but there was one massive, gaping hole in his CV and robust ego: the title of chief executive officer.

He knew the opportunity would come, but now at thirty-eight years old, he had only a few more years to hit his self-imposed deadline. And Valley Alley never missed a freaking deadline. Ever.

Alley and I shook hands, and he gestured for me to have a seat. Before sitting down, he ran his hands down his blue cotton shirt to smooth out the wrinkles. I'm sure it was just a habit because that never works, does it? As he lowered his long body into the chair, he easily and casually chatted with me, inquiring about my trip, my family, my experience living in San Diego—the usual stuff that any friendly person would want to know, or at least pretend to.

"I know that Janice thinks very highly of you," he said, shifting the conversation around to the purpose of our meeting. "Especially because she sent you up here to check me out before she makes a final decision about bringing me on board." He chuckled.

"Well, I'm happy to do it," I said. "And I'm honored that she puts that kind of faith in me, but I'm really just a sounding board for her."

Eye contact came easily to Alley. He met my gaze through his stylish black round-framed glasses. I knew he was thirty-eight, but he could easily have passed for thirty, which was a little surprising, given the business mileage he had already accrued in his storied career. I thought the wear-and-tear would show with a few more wrinkles on his face, or a dash of gray in his hair. Instead, smooth tanned skin, dark red-brown hair, and the proverbial eye twinkle all indicated a chill guy with his life on cruise control, which it most certainly was not.

With very little prompting on my part, he spoke easily about his life and aspirations. He was named after his grandfather, Sir Allistair Langstrom, who was a British nobleman, philanthropist, and, despite his title, a bit of a social activist. Alley never knew his grandfather, but he was proud of the legacy and fancied himself a philanthropist, too. He donated to a children's charity every year, and it seemed to me that he was very proud of that fact. I made a mental note that he and Janice might be aligned in their mutual care for our younger generation and that this could facilitate a deeper connection between them. I also knew that many people donate to charity because they feel they have to, not because they want to. I got the distinct feeling that he truly cared.

He loved his sister, who lived in Minnesota, and he called his parents back in Boston every weekend without fail. He had no wife, no life partner, no kids, and no plans to change any of that, at least not in the near future.

"To borrow the old cliché," he said, "I'm married to my career. I do have friends, though," he laughed.

"How would your friends describe you?" I asked.

Impressively, he didn't hesitate.

"They would tell you that I'm a good friend, I think. They can count on me in a pinch. I like to laugh and have a good time. They'd tell you that I'm generous, but they'd also describe me as being a little self-centered. Not selfish—self-centered. Meaning that I'm ambitious to the point that I prioritize my business results and effectiveness over more frivolous, social stuff, for example. But they'd excuse that in me because they know it's a necessary evil to be successful in the Valley culture. They know that I want to make my mark on this world, and I believe that they're rooting for me."

"Nice," I said, ever the eloquent one.

We chatted for over an hour, and I enjoyed the ease of our conversation, his thoughtful response to my inquiries, his sparkling intelligence, and the rapport that we'd rapidly built together. My impression for Janice: *This guy is a keeper; snatch him up for the COO position.*

"One last two-part question for you, if you don't mind," I said, glancing at my watch to assure myself that I wouldn't miss my flight home.

"Fire away," said Alley with a smile.

"Well," I said. "My leadership philosophy—which Janice and XinoniX share, by the way, and which originally came from the founder's dad—is 'Do what you love in the service of people who love what you do.'"

"So I understand," he said.

"Part one: What do you think of that? And part two: What's *your* leadership philosophy?"

"Got it. My answer to part one is, I think it's nice. *Love* is an unusual word in business, but I get it. I think you're asking me because you want to know if I can get behind it, and the answer is yes. Yes, I can. I also know about the LEAP values—Love, Energy, Audacity, and Proof—and I can support those, too."

"Great," I said. "You're right; it's important to Janice and everyone else that you believe in their approach to doing business. And part two?"

"I have two philosophies," Alley held up two fingers. "*Do well by doing good*, and . . ." he paused for effect. "*It's not personal; it's business*."

Interesting, I thought as I rose from my chair. *That's a little cold.*

I've always regarded business as a very personal endeavor, but maybe I misunderstood his sentiment. The nuances were worth exploring, so I placed a kind of mental asterisk on my thought and set it aside as something worth revisiting later. Clearly, we could have had several more hours of conversation on this topic alone, but that would have to wait for another day because I had a flight to catch.

We shook hands as I rose from my chair, and he pulled me in for a quick bro hug.

"Been a pleasure," he said.

"Pleasure was all mine, Alley. I suspect you'll be hearing from Janice soon. I know that moving down to San Diego would be a big deal, but, if all works out, I think you'll be happy jumping aboard the XinoniX love train."

He laughed. "I'm sure I would."

We said our goodbyes. And now, as I recall that scene with the benefit of 20/20 hindsight, my guess is that Valley Alley watched me disappear through the door of the Chat Bar, laughed to himself, and rolled his eyes.

CHAPTER 3

Later, on a sparkling San Diego morning, Alastair Langstrom arrived in the corporate office of XinoniX. He stepped through the front doors to see a banner display stretching across the lobby wall that read *Welcome, Alley!* in big, bold, colorful letters. Janice was waiting there to meet him, and then she walked him around the floor and introduced him to each person, one by one. By all accounts, he was kind, gracious, and attentive to everyone. It was a stellar first impression all the way around, which immediately cut through a lot of the usual new-sheriff-in-town anxiety that's par for the course in most situations like this. He settled into his newly decorated, finely appointed office and the honeymoon period appeared to be off to a stellar start.

He spent the next several weeks in student mode, learning all he could about the current business, its culture, and its people, as well as systems, policies, procedures, and all various and sundry things that made the company tick. From what Janice had told me at the time, everything was going just swimmingly, which made me happy and, frankly, a bit relieved, since I'd recommended him so highly to her and the rest of her senior team.

"He's a find," I'd told them with utmost confidence. "You can't go wrong with this one."

But soon enough, the rumblings began.

"He's asking a lot of questions about our values," Jimmy Sun in finance confided in me one day when I was there to visit with Janice. A meeting that, I gathered from her vacant office, she had apparently forgotten about.

"Well . . . that's a good thing, isn't it? Sounds like he's wanting to get clarity, right?" I asked as we walked together down the hall.

Jimmy looked dubious. "He called it 'that love crap,'" he said.

"Oh." Alarm bells jangled in the deep recesses of my brain. "There was probably a better way for him to say that," I said with a forced smile.

Inside, I felt myself churn. Those didn't sound like the words from a guy who'd told me—and I'm quoting him here—"you want to know if I can get behind it, and the answer is yes" when I'd asked him specifically about that so-called "love crap."

But I thought maybe Jimmy and I were overreacting, so I brushed it off and moved on.

And then just a few hours later, I received a short text message from Bob Jeffers, the former XinoniX CEO, who had tapped Janice to succeed him just before he retired and moved away to Palm Springs. Jeffers had undergone a massive leadership transformation from renowned jerk to inspiring executive (facilitated, in part, by a panic attack that felt like a massive heart failure and terrified him into reevaluating his life and relationships) and finished his career as a stellar exemplar of the company's LEAP values. It was very unusual for him to reach out, happy as he was to be living unencumbered in the perpetual sauna of the California desert.

"Read that Langstrom is new COO," his first text said.

"Yup," I'd replied.

"You can't trust him."

And that was that. No explanation. No follow-up commentary. And no response to my request for clarification.

Those four little words—*You can't trust him*—were enough to water and fertilize my existing seed of doubt so that it instantaneously sprouted and spread like a crazed kudzu in my chest.

Trust is a fragile thing. The conventional wisdom is that it's something that you must earn. And while that may generally be true, my natural tendency is to trust first. As a colleague of mine said to me recently, "Trust isn't something that you earn; it's a gift that you give. Distrust is something that you earn." That describes me to a tee. I'll give you my trust right out of the gate, and you'll either live up to that gift or earn my distrust by lying to me, by manipulating a situation to suit yourself at my own or others' expense, or by simply not doing what you said you would do. Bob Jeffers's short, ominous missive put me on high alert, and even though I didn't want to create unnecessary concern, I knew I would have to talk to Janice about this. That was the kind of relationship we had, and my saying nothing ran the risk of all this coming back to bite us if my concern turned out to be well-founded.

Which, as you'll soon see, it was.

CHAPTER 4

The next day, I met Janice for lunch at the Wake-Up Call in Encinitas, our favorite diner. I loved their food and service, but more importantly, it had great sentimental value for me. The Wake-Up Call had been started and owned by the late Agnes Golden, an accomplished entrepreneur whose wisdom about business and life had had a great impact on me when I'd met her here almost twenty years ago—at the very table where Janice and I were sitting, it suddenly occurred to me. I gave myself permission to bask in Agnes's memory for a moment. Among her many stellar attributes, Agnes had been a master of balancing radical, tough honesty with kindness—a skill I hoped to draw on today. With that in mind, I turned my full attention to Janice just as our food arrived.

Given that Janice had put a great deal of hope and money into Alley, I knew this would be a delicate conversation. And there was something else I needed to discuss with her, too. I chose to take a casual "oh, by the way" approach to the subject. After our usual quasi-smalltalk and general catch-up stuff, I started guiding the conversation with an innocent question.

"So . . . how's it going with Alley? Everything cool so far?" I asked as I picked a french fry off her plate.

"Great!" she chirped without hesitation. "I haven't been around much lately—some nonprofit stuff I've been dealing with—but by all accounts, he's doing a great job."

"Good, good. That's great. Really great," I said.

"What?" said Janice. She knew me so well. And I have a lousy face for poker.

"Well, it's just that I've been hearing some talk that at least a few people may be questioning his sincerity a bit."

"Really?" She chuckled dismissively. "That's probably just because they're still getting to know him. After all, he hasn't been here very long. I'm not concerned," she said, waving her hand in the air as if to brush the subject away.

But when I told her about the text from Bob Jeffers, her demeanor shifted.

"Really?" This time, no chuckle. "Why would he send a message like that?" She was clearly irritated.

"I don't know; he didn't give me much to go on," I said. "But he's obviously concerned. I can't imagine he has an ulterior motive, can you?"

"No . . . but still. Stirring up doubt like that—it just doesn't seem right."

"May I make a suggestion, Janice?" I asked.

"Of course. Always."

"I know you're excited about your education project. It's a great thing, and I'm happy that you're doing it . . ."

"But?"

"But, to put it bluntly, you're spending too much time away from the business. You made a promise to the company that you'd carry the culture torch, and you can't do that in absentia. Especially now in Alley's early days. You need to be present."

So much for my casual, indirect approach.

"Rumor and innuendo don't help anyone," I continued. "So you need to get firsthand knowledge of what's going on and throw yourself back into the thick of it. Be there to help Alley adjust to the team, and them to him."

"Okay, I hear you. I'll do that."

"Cool," I said, unconvincingly.

"What else?" She could see the concern still wrinkling around my eyebrows.

I hesitated to answer but recalling the spirit of Agnes Golden and her signature blunt honesty, I gave myself permission to be direct with my dear client and—more significantly—my friend.

"Frankly, Janice, I've been hearing some grumblings about you, too."

She looked startled.

"Like what?" she said, with a hint of hurt in her voice.

"Well . . . your folks clearly love you. That's for sure. And your credibility with them, after all you've been through together, is still strong."

"But I need to be around more," Janice interjected. "I get it."

"Yes, and . . ." I paused.

"What?" She was starting to get a little miffed with my obvious reluctance to say what was on my mind.

"Your follow-through isn't . . . well, it isn't what it used to be. Several folks told me about a virtual meeting that you were invited to and didn't show up for."

"I apologized for that," she said softly.

"Yes, I heard that, too," I said. "But apparently that kind of thing has happened more than once with several people on your team." I listed a few of the incidents as evidence, including the recent meeting she'd missed with me.

"I know I'm not perfect," she said, defensively. "But I really don't think it's happening as often as you're making it out to be."

"Well, you may think it's not, but that doesn't matter. What I do know is that perception is reality, and, without a doubt, your perceived lack of follow-through is having a noticeable impact on the team."

"How do you know that?" She leaned in, challenging my statement with her rather obvious body language.

"Because they have a name for it."

"A name?"

"They call it 'pulling a Janice,'" I said.

"Oh," she said, looking defeated. "Wow. I don't know what to say."

Her voice trailed off, and I felt her deflating.

"This is totally fixable, Janice," I said, trying to lift her spirits. "It's a really simple problem to remedy, isn't it? You just have to pay more attention to the words you say and the commitments you make."

She nodded.

"And it all starts with you being around more, so you can shore up the relationship weaknesses that are starting and mend the ones that have already been damaged."

"Okay. You're right. And I'll commit to doing that," she said with a forced smile.

"Fantastic!" I said and took one last bite of my ginormous turkey club sandwich.

"Starting next month," she said.

And that's when I heard that little Scooby-Doo voice in my head.

"Ruh-roh," it said.

CHAPTER 5

Some people believe that everything happens for a reason. Others chalk up life's circumstances to chance, as if we're all bouncing around like so many billiard balls and, if we're lucky, sometimes the perfect shot just lines up. Then all you need is the skill to sink that sucker in the pocket. I'm not going to tell you what to believe, but in any case, it seemed like exquisite timing when, right after my lunch with Janice, I heard that my longtime mentors Jim Kouzes and Barry Posner were visiting San Diego to present at a conference.

Although Jim and I had spoken several times in recent years, it had been a while since I'd seen either him or Barry, and I was excited to sit in the same room with the two of them and breathe the same oxygen, which still felt like a great luxury in these post-COVID days. And, since I felt a storm brewing on the XinoniX front, I really wanted to get their take on the situation.

I met them in the lobby of the Intercontinental Hotel on the bay in the Columbia neighborhood of downtown San Diego, and we walked out to a small coffee stand on the boardwalk just outside the building.

I always felt short walking next to these guys, not only physically because they're both several inches taller than my five-foot-ten-inch frame, but also metaphorically because of their towering wisdom in the field—a notion they would readily eschew. They have different senses of humor—Barry's being particularly dry and Jim's gentler—but they share a deep sense of humility and deference to the talents of others, including mine.

We settled at a table facing the water under the shade of a thick Canary palm. We played congenial catch-up for several minutes while we sipped at our coffees and enjoyed the sweet San Diego breeze blowing in from across the bay. As our conversation turned to business and career updates, I took the opportunity to bring them up to speed on Janice, Alley, XinoniX, and my concerns about all of the above.

And in recounting the situation to them, I realized I had a higher-level, existential question that had been subtly gnawing at me lately.

Even though Kouzes and Posner weren't household names like, say, Einstein or Beyoncé, their research on credibility was legendary among leadership geeks in many businesses and academic institutions the world over. As B-school professors and business consultants, they'd published untold numbers of research papers and several books, most notably

The Leadership Challenge and *Credibility*. I had referenced these guys countless times over the years, their acronymic phrase, *DWYSYWD*—pronounced Dwi-zee-wid and standing for *Do What You Say You Will Do*—being the term I had quoted most often by far.

Do What You Say You Will Do. Seven little words that seem so obvious, so simple to understand, and yet, in my experience both personally and professionally, so challenging to put into practice. But that congruence between one's words and actions—or the lack thereof—describes the essence of a person's credibility with others. So I started with that.

"Does DWYSYWD still matter as much as it used to?" I asked them both.

"Meaning?" asked Barry.

"I mean, it's like we're living in a world where, it seems to me, we've accepted it as normal when people don't tell the truth. It's like we're just fine with that. And if we're okay with that, then aren't we also becoming more tolerant of people who don't follow through on their words, their commitments? I'm not sure I'm saying this right. I guess what I'm asking is . . . why should DWYSYWD matter to me, or to anyone, in these very strange times?" I paused to gather my thoughts.

"It's a great question," said Barry.

"Let me give it a whirl," said Jim, his eyes crinkling in a smile. "In the world we're in today—or yesterday, or tomorrow, for that matter—we play the game of life with a 'three strikes and you're out' rule."

"Really? A baseball analogy?" Barry playfully soft-punched his partner on the shoulder. "I hear you struck out in T-ball."

Old friends for sure. Barry loved giving Jim the occasional teasing poke. Jim ignored him and continued.

"The first time I don't do what I say I will do—like I miss a Zoom call or a meeting that you're counting on me for, you'll likely extend me a little grace, give me the benefit of the doubt. Shit happens to everyone, right? Life jumps up and disrupts you. Kids get sick, you get sick, something happens, and even though you intend to, you can't follow through. Or you make a mistake. We all make mistakes, so we're all likely to forgive someone else's. Maybe I just screwed up. Maybe I put the wrong day on my calendar, or the wrong time zone on the right day."

"Yeah. I've done that," I said.

"Of course you have. Because you're not perfect, and neither am I. And neither is Barry. No human being is perfect."

"But . . ." said Barry.

"But," Jim continued. "If it happens again—the second time I don't do what I say I will do, the second time I miss our call . . ."

"Now it's becoming a problem," Barry interjected.

"Now it's becoming a problem," Jim repeated, shooting Barry a look. "That's strike two. So let's say you gave me a second chance after I missed our first call. I'm still in the game with you—I'm still at bat—but now that I've missed another one, you're just not sure about me. You're a little suspicious. You're less convinced that you can count on me in the future. But you're still giving me the benefit of the doubt. You know that I'm a busy guy; I have a lot on my plate. I'm trying to handle a lot of things, and maybe I just overpromised. Even though you're irritated, you'll likely forgive me for the second strike."

"True," I said.

"But if it happens a third time? Strike three, and I'm out. I've broken a trust, a bond in our relationship, and I'm in a deep hole with you now in terms of my believability. After that, if I tell you I'm going to do something, anything—the service I promised, the project I said I'd deliver, the budget numbers I said I'd hit—you're just not going to believe that I will."

"And our relationship is done?" I asked.

"Or at least severely damaged," Barry answered with a more serious tone.

"In your eyes, our relationship is damaged or maybe even destroyed—depending on your tolerance level," said Jim. "But me? I can repeat that behavior with someone else, can't I?"

"Instead of learning a lesson about yourself and trying to correct it, you just move on?"

"Right, Steve. I can move on to a different person and go through that same process. But where is that going to get me? How many business relationships am I going to have in my life? How many marriages can I have? How many problems with my kids can I have before they just throw up their hands and say, *Yeah, yeah, blah, blah—you say that, but you never follow through*?"

"I imagine it's different for everyone," I said, thinking out loud. "But why don't people follow through? I mean, I guess that sometimes it's intentional. Sometimes people make promises that they have no intention of keeping."

"Yes," said Barry, his brow furrowed. "That's called lying. And, like you said a few minutes ago, it's a chronic problem these days, for sure. But for now, let's assume that they're not being malicious. Something happens—either within or outside of their control—and they don't deliver as promised. The very basis of trust gets broken or even shattered to smithereens. And, depending on the stakes of the specific circumstance, it can happen in an instant. If I don't come through on something that's really important to you, that you're really counting on me for, I won't get the luxury of two more strikes."

"Something a lot more consequential than missing a phone call," I said, reflecting on how many times I'd done that over the years.

"In any case," Barry went on, "if you really want to have a deep human relationship, there has to be trust, agreed?"

"Of course," I said.

"And since you're a business leadership kind of guy, Steve, you know that all of this is true on an organizational level, too. As customers—or potential customers—do we trust a company's product? Do we trust the service? Do we trust the invoice? The brand promise? And it's quite clear what happens when the answer is no. We take our business elsewhere, perhaps forever."

"So, companies—like individual people—need to Do What They Say They Will Do . . . DWTSTWD." It sounded like *dwitstwid* when I said it.

"Yes," Barry continued, "it's the same dynamic for individuals and organizations. But in either case, it's not exactly symmetrical."

"Meaning what?" I asked.

"Meaning you may get some points for being trustworthy, but you lose a whole *boatload* of points when you break that trust. I have a friend who went to the same gas station for years—*years*. And then one day, an employee mistreated her in some way. I'm not even sure of the details—just that she felt deeply disrespected. And guess what? She never went there again. To this day, she'll go out of her way and even pay more somewhere else just to *not* go back to that place. And she told me about it, and now I'm telling you, and who knows how many people you'll tell. And let's not forget about her venting her spleen on Yelp and Google. And for all she knows that guy who dissed her may be long gone. Hell, the place may even be under new ownership."

"So the one time they fell way short of their service promise negated all those years of having delivered? Don't you think she overreacted a bit?" I asked, nervously scanning my own history to determine whether I'd ever committed such an offense with my clients.

"That's not for me to say," said Barry. "That's her experience, and as a customer she has a right to respond that way. The point is, that's just a local gas station, but the lesson is that we all have to be supremely mindful of doing what we say we will do, because there can be severe consequences when we screw it up, even once, intentionally or otherwise, individually and organizationally."

"And to put it all together," added Jim, "as an individual leader in a company, as someone whose job it is to set the example for others, to represent a group of people, I personally need to Do What We Say We Will Do—DWWSWWD."

"That's even harder to say," I laughed, trying again to sound the acronym out as a word.

"Hah! Right! It's hard to say," Jim said, "but even harder to do. As a leader of a team, I personally—no matter what challenges we may face—need to be the walking, talking, living, breathing example of the standards, values, promises, and behaviors that *we* say are important around here."

None of this was new to me, of course. Like I said, these guys were my mentors and their body of work deeply informed and inspired my own. But, considering what I saw happening with Janice, it was all hitting me at a deeper level. I needed to help her bridge the gap between understanding the idea of DWYSYWD—which is easy to do—and putting it into practice every day. And that wasn't going to happen until she held herself personally accountable to her own words as an individual and the company's collective words—that is, their LEAP values—as a leader.

"Accountability" is a word we hear a lot these days. I typically hear it used as *that thing that we desperately want other people to take.* "These people need to be more accountable," is a proclamation I've heard more times than I care to recall. And while it may be true that "they" need to be accountable, it seemed to me that this whole consideration came down to holding oneself accountable—ridiculously accountable—to living up to one's own promises.

And as I considered the implications of that idea, I found myself struggling with the practicality of it all. I shared my troubled thoughts with the guys.

"I've been around for over six decades now, and I'm embarrassed to say that it's taken me so long to figure this out," I began. "People who consistently follow through on their words, who do what they say they will do, are exceedingly rare."

"Do you really think so?" asked Barry, running his hand over his gray mustache.

"I do," I said. "I don't think it's a willful or malicious thing, in most cases. I know it's not the case with me. Maybe it's because no matter how well-intentioned I may be, I often let my words fly out of my mouth with reckless abandon without realizing that the person I'm talking to is hearing me with critical precision. I think I'm just spewing words, or maybe thinking out loud; they're hearing a commitment, a pledge, a vow to follow up and deliver. And when I don't come through on that pledge that I didn't know I took, that person's trust in me drops a notch."

I turned to Jim. "I say to you, for example, 'Hey, Jim! Maybe we should write a book together,' because I think that would be nice, I'd enjoy it, and I'm feeling particularly energetic and creative in this moment. Chances are, however, that you're hearing, 'We will write a book together.' And when you don't hear from me next week, or month, or year, your trust in me takes a hit, right?"

"Maybe a little," Jim smiled.

"Right. We're back to strike one. The problem is that I am completely and blissfully unaware of my decline. And I think that's true for all of us: Every time we say something, it seems, we create an expectation in others' minds and hearts—whether we mean to or not. And given that none of us is perfect, we're constantly setting ourselves up for earning another's distrust."

Pulling a Janice, I mused to myself.

We kicked this back and forth for a while, and we agreed that DWYSYWD is not about being perfect. It *is* about acknowledging that even though we'll never achieve perfect consistency between our words and our actions, we should strive for it anyway. And it all starts with our awareness of our own words and actions and how all of that is being perceived by others.

As we talked though all of this together, we found ourselves immersed in a burst of collective creativity, which I guess is not all that unusual when you put a bunch of writers together. And from this spontaneous co-creative jam session among the three of us, a personal declaration, a manifesto of sorts, soon emerged. It took the form of a challenge, a promise for each of us to rise to—one that I believed would serve us all if we truly embraced it in our lives. We massaged the words for a few minutes, and, fearing that it would all dissipate into the ether as soon as we departed, I had the presence of mind to write it all down on—you guessed it—the back of a napkin.

We called it The Radical Promise:

> *I embrace the reality that doing what you say you will do is not just important, it is imperative; therefore, I make a Radical Promise to hold myself 100% accountable to my own words. DWYSYWD is not a platitude. It's not a truism. It's a deep, soul-based commitment to the authentic core of who I am. All of this requires a significantly heightened sense of self-awareness, where I truly think before I speak. And once I speak, I know that it is not acceptable to retract. Having said that, I acknowledge that I am not perfect—no one is. I recognize that this is an impossible standard to live up to in an absolute and literal sense. But it is a truly significant, monumental aspiration to have for myself, because in the striving to live up to it, I create a much higher rate of consistency between my words and my actions. And that's all I can ask of myself as a fallible human being. Once I have established that standard for myself, it gives me the credibility to ask the same of others—which I fully intend to do.*

In reading this back to Jim and Barry, I felt the full import and personal implications of the words. I mean, it was fun and inspiring to put it together and all that, but hearing them come out of my own mouth—in the first person, no less—well, that was a much hotter kettle of fish. What had I just subscribed to? Was I ready and willing to commit to such a high bar in the way I showed up in the world?

"Holy shmoly," I whispered. "This is terrifying."

They laughed.

"That's what makes it radical, isn't it?" Barry said.

Yes, it was a scary proposition—but for all the right reasons. I realized how excited I felt, and I wanted to share it with anyone who would listen. I imagined printing leaflets and dropping them from airplanes over every major business center in the world. Yeah, I tend to get carried away with the audacious vision thing.

"I can't wait to give this to Janice," I said, narrowing my scope a bit.

"Well, then you better be ready," said Barry, adjusting his glasses in thought.

"Yes . . . you know what you need to do first, don't you, Farber?" Jim asked with a mischievous smile.

"DWWSWWD," said Barry.

"Lead by example," added Jim.

"Walk your talk; practice what you preach," Barry continued.

"Never write a check with your mouth that your body can't cash," Jim exclaimed.

"Model the way," they said together.

"Okay!" I laughed. "I get it." I pulled at my collar, Rodney Dangerfield style. "You guys are relentless."

"And," said Jim, "if she takes this seriously . . ."

"She will," I interjected.

". . . then it's going to stir up a lot of stuff for her and raise a lot of questions about how to live up to that promise. But I think you're fully capable of helping her with that."

"Agreed," Barry said.

I wasn't quite so sure. I reread the words on the napkin.

"Yeah, well . . . maybe you guys should be on call just in case," I said, only half-kidding.

"Any time," they said almost in unison.

And it's a good thing they meant it.

CHAPTER 6

The next day, Janice sat at her desk and rubbed her temples as she read the words on the paper in front of her. As I watched her, I reflected on how little she'd changed since we'd first met over two decades ago. She was in her mid-twenties back then, a talented young executive on the fast track to a bright future. Sure, she looked a little older now—she had a few more lines around her dark brown eyes, and gray streaks ran through her hair, which was a little less black than it used to be. But she still radiated the same youthful energy and warm, genuine smile that naturally drew people in when they first met her. Sadly, her smile wasn't appearing as often these last few days.

I had transferred the words from the napkin to a legal pad and handed the sheet to Janice when I'd sat down in her office a few minutes before. She tapped her fingers on the paper and sighed as she looked out the window at the dramatic orange sunset spreading over the clear San Diego sky.

"Pulling a Janice," she mused out loud, obviously comparing those words to the ones she'd just read.

"That really got to you, didn't it?" I asked, softly.

"I can't shake it," she said, moving her gaze from the window to meet mine.

I made a mental note that she seemed more bothered by fears about her own reputation than she was by the rumors about Alley. She hadn't mentioned him once since I'd brought that concern to her attention. That didn't worry me. As a leader, she needed to focus on her own credibility as her first order of business. She needed to repair the cracks in her own foundation before it crumbled underneath her.

She picked the paper up from her desk and waved it in front of her.

"This . . ." she said, with a wistful, half-smile on her face.

"Pushes your buttons a bit," I offered.

"Like a starving rat pushing for pellets."

"Lovely image," I laughed. "I know exactly what you mean. Same for me."

"Even though you co-wrote it."

"Especially because of that," I said.

"I don't know," she sighed. "It seems like an impossibly high bar. *To hold myself 100% accountable to my own words,"* she read from the paper.

I let the silence settle in around us as she considered the immense challenge of such a radical promise. Knowing Janice as I did, I had anticipated her resistance, and, to my credit, I had the foresight to arrange something special to help her through it. And, judging from the angle of the setting sun, happy hour at a certain local establishment was nigh.

"C'mon," I said, pushing my chair back and jumping to my feet. "Let's get out of here. There's someone I want you to meet."

CHAPTER 7

Cat Cassidy closed out her happy hour set at Boudin's Louisiana Bar and Grill with a screaming slide guitar solo. *Her band was even tighter than usual,* I thought. *And she just gets better and better.* Under the stage lights, her tight-knit hair, which was dyed golden blonde, shone in contrast to the light brown skin on her youthful face. Maybe it was because of her gravelly voice and talent for slide guitar, but she'd always reminded me of a younger, African American version of Bonnie Raitt. And there was one other very notable difference: I'm sure that Bonnie didn't have a six-inch-tall full-color rendering of the Cat in the Hat tattooed on her right calf like Catherine Cassidy does. Even after a decade and a half, it always made me smile.

Janice and I walked over to meet her as she stepped off the stage.

Cat was not only a fabulous musician, but a remarkable CEO as well. I'd known her for fifteen years now—almost as long as I'd known Janice—and I reflected on how fast that time had flashed by. She ran a staffing company called YSC and, like Janice, had built a people-oriented culture that was the envy of her industry. At the core of their corporate DNA was a practice they called *Greater Than Yourself*—*GTY*—which encouraged everyone to invest in one another for the purpose of making everyone the best at what they do. Consequently, the best in the business flocked to YSC. And since her employees were her best recruiters (*You HAVE to work here* was their common value proposition when talking to people about their experience), Cat spent zero dollars on outside headhunters.

Oddly enough, even though they were both high-powered C-suite women in the San Diego community, Cat and Janice had never met. And I was thrilled that it was finally happening right before my eyes. Over the years, I had regaled each of them with stories about the other, and, to my sheer delight, their connection was warm and immediate as they embraced each other in a spontaneous hug.

"Well, it's about time!" exclaimed Cat.

"It sure is," said Janice, clasping Cat's hands in hers. "And, wow, your guitar playing is off the chain!"

As they talked, I stepped away to greet the two men sitting in the shadows at a corner table in the back of the room.

"Gentlemen," I said as I approached the table.

"You were right," said Jim. "She's excellent."

Barry smiled and nodded in agreement.

I knew that Jim would appreciate Cat's artistry. He was a music lover. In fact, he was the one who had introduced me to the music of Steve Earle a couple of decades before, and I had immediately become a raving fan.

But the music was a bonus, a wrapping on the package of the bigger intent of the evening.

"Thanks again for agreeing to do this, guys. It's going to mean a lot to the both of them." I cocked a thumb in the direction of the stage. I leaned over the table and whispered conspiratorially, "They're huge fans of yours."

"I promise we'll be nice," Barry winked.

I had given both Janice and Cat signed copies of *The Leadership Challenge* many, many years ago, and each still had the book displayed prominently on their respective shelves.

"And," I wiggled my eyebrows, "they have no idea that you're here."

I could barely contain my mischievous enthusiasm as I went back to corral the new friends and escort them back to the table where, ever gracious, the two men were standing to greet them.

"Janice Everson, Cat Cassidy," I said. "Meet Jim Kouzes and Barry Posner."

Oh, yeah, I thought as I gleefully watched the shocked reaction on the women's faces. *This was gonna be good.*

I left the four of them to get acquainted and stepped over to the bar to order a round of beers for the table. As I waited for the bartender, I mused on how to get this conversation going in the right direction. I wasn't sure that Janice was really grasping the full implication of her waning reputation, and I wanted her to take her own credibility challenge seriously. I figured that my two ringers, along with Cat, would be able to inspire Janice in ways that I couldn't. Or at the very least, they could bring the additional *oomph* that she'd need to commit to the promise. But I also didn't want her to feel like I'd lured her into some kind of trap; I didn't want her to feel like this was an intervention, though in a way it was. So all I had to do was delicately steer the chat in the direction of Jim and Barry's credibility research and maybe she'd get the personal implications. As I walked back to the table, I still wasn't sure how this was going to play out.

". . . pulling a Janice," I heard Janice say as I sat down with the group. "That's what they're calling it."

I raised my eyebrows in surprise. Sounded like Janice had just jumped right into the river without me. This was going to be a lot easier than I thought. I chuckled out loud.

"What's so funny?" said Janice, giving me *the look*.

"Nothing. Sorry. Nothing at all," I smiled. "Just musing on how *guarded* you are," I said, with affectionate sarcasm.

"Hey," she said with a laugh. "This is freaking Kouzes and Posner right here. I'm not going to waste a second of this opportunity."

And she didn't. She took a few more minutes to tell everyone about her current situation at XinoniX, her non-profit work, and a few other details so they had the full context of her challenge as she currently understood it.

"Well, Janice," said Jim, "first of all, thank you for your willingness to share all of that with us. We're honored that you've entrusted us with your story."

"Indeed, we are," added Barry. "We know it's not an easy thing."

"No, it's not," added Cat. "I'm inspired by your candor, too."

"The thing is," said Jim, "this is all about your team's belief in you, Janice. And, simply put, if they don't believe in the messenger, they won't believe the message."

"Whatever the message is," said Barry.

Wow, I thought, *right for the jugular, huh, fellas?*

CHAPTER 8

Even though Janice had already shared her personal challenge and invited the group's input, I had a feeling that we should first step back to a higher, more universal level of context for this discussion. I asked Jim to talk a little bit about the research he and Barry had done and how they had come to their messenger/message conclusion.

Barry sat up a little straighter in his chair, and Jim's face lit up at the request. He didn't literally rub his hands together in a *goody-goody* kind of way, but he might as well have. That's how much these guys loved their work.

"Here's what we did," Jim began. "We started out by asking people to answer a simple, personal question: 'What do you look for and admire in a leader—someone whose direction you would willingly follow?'"

"The key word being *willingly*," added Barry. "Not someone you *had* to follow because they were signing your paycheck or had your life in their hands."

"Right," Jim continued. "And over time, we've asked that question of people in virtually all industries, in both the public and private sector, on every continent on the planet."

"Every. Continent. On the planet," I reiterated with overly dramatic emphasis. It's what I do.

"And what emerged were several characteristics of an admired leader that hold universally true across the board," said Jim.

"And what would you guess is in the number-one slot?" Barry asked Janice, demonstrating his professorial side.

"I'll go with 'honesty,'" Janice answered. "At least, that's what I would say."

"And you'd be right," Jim continued. "First and foremost, people need to believe you're honest, that you're trustworthy, that you have integrity. Number two on the list is competence or expertise, that you have the skills and abilities to do the things you say you will do, and to do the job that you have in front of you."

"So . . . honest and competent are the top two characteristics of an admired leader," I summarized.

"Yes. And here's what that means. When you compare our findings to the research on source credibility—the study of what makes the source of a message credible—you find a direct equivalency. The source credibility discussion has been going on since the 1940s, but we can put it simply like this: A communicator is perceived as credible when they're seen as being trustworthy and having expertise. Do you see the parallel?"

"I think so," said Janice.

"Let's compare," said Jim. "For the leadership characteristic *honest*, you could say trustworthy; for *competent*, you could say expertise."

"Therefore," Barry jumped in, "when you put it all together, the number-one thing we look for and admire in a leader we would willingly follow is credibility."

"So," I said, trying to weave the threads of our conversation, "when I see a person as credible, I'm more likely to believe what they're saying. When that person is also a leader, I'm more likely to follow them, too."

"Right," said Jim. "And after credibility, the next leadership characteristic that rises to the top is 'inspiring' or 'dynamic.' Being inspiring and uplifting lets people know you have the fire in your heart to make your message a reality, to follow through on your words. If you lose that dynamism, that energy for your values and beliefs, you just won't come across as a leader who really believes what she's saying."

In their typical back-and-forth style, Jim and Barry went on to explain that what usually takes the fourth slot after honest, competent, and inspiring is *forward-looking*, otherwise known as the vision thing. If a person is choosing to follow you, they'll need to experience you as a credible leader with a clear idea of the destination to which you're leading them.

And with that, we landed right back where we started. "If you don't believe in the messenger, you won't believe the message," I reiterated.

"Some call it the *Kouzes-Posner First Law of Leadership*," said Jim.

I hadn't heard that before. "You guys have a law named after you?" I exclaimed. "What do I have to do to get a law?" I was thinking that *Farber's First Law of Smart-Assery* would be a good candidate.

"In any event," Barry continued without acknowledging my question, which he had apparently regarded as rhetorical, "all of this means that your credibility, Janice—and this is true for everyone—is ultimately a very personal thing. And what that credibility looks like, simply put, is DWYSYWD."

"Do what you say you will do," said Janice quietly, almost to herself.

"In other words, what do you *say* is important, and what do you *do* to demonstrate your belief in that importance? That's the key question for every leader," said Jim.

I could see that Janice was letting this sink in way down deep. All of this seemed simple and so patently obvious from the 25,000-foot view. But it was easy to overlook in the moment. And, after all, life is really just a series of moments, isn't it?

"So I need to give people a reason to believe in me," Janice said out loud.

"Every single day," Cat said softly, putting her hand on Janice's arm. "Whenever I'm faced with a challenge, my first response is always to check to see if I still believe in myself. Do I believe I have the capability to meet and rise above it?

And do I believe that the cause I've been engaged in—whatever it is—is still worthwhile? Repeatedly, it seems, I have to reclarify what's important to me. That's where it always starts—for me, anyway. And then I check to see if I believe that this cause—again, whatever it is—is going to be good for my team, my company, my clients, and the various stakeholders I'm responsible for leading. Once I've established all of that, then I check to see if my own actions are lining up with and demonstrating that belief."

"Very well put," said Jim.

Cat blushed a little. "I'm not saying it's easy," she said, trying to deflect the compliment.

"So you're constantly checking your own actions to see if they line up with your words?" asked Janice, sounding a touch incredulous.

"And to see if they align with my beliefs and values," said Cat.

"That's a lot of checking on yourself." Janice looked around the table for confirmation of her concern. "It sounds overwhelming," she said, looking at Cat. "How on earth do you manage that and get anything else done?"

"Great question," chuckled Jim. "I'd like to know, too."

"I could use a little more checking my own damn self," I piped in.

"Okay, Cat," said Barry. "Looks like you're up. Tell us how you do it."

CHAPTER 9

A black backpack slung around his shoulders, Jimmy Sun pulled his bike up to the XinoniX building, hopped off, and tucked his helmet under his arm. As he carried his ride through the doors and into the elevator, he felt the butterflies flapping in his gut. Alley had asked him for an update on several finance matters, and he was about to sit down for his very first one-on-one with the new COO.

He had enjoyed working from home during the pandemic shutdown, but Jimmy was happy to be around actual live human beings again. Most of these folks he liked a whole lot—and some he loved and counted as dear friends—but he still wasn't sure what to make of Alley.

XinoniX was Jimmy's first and only job since he'd graduated from San Diego State, so he didn't really have a prior experience for comparison. What he did know was that this company had given him a shot right out of the gate and that meant the world to him.

This place was not a steppingstone in Jimmy's career; he intended to be a lifer. He would continue to do great work and develop himself to contribute more and more for as long as Janice and the team would have him. And their shared values? Well, that was more important to him than anything. Which was why he was so alarmed when he heard Alley refer to "that love crap."

Jimmy and I felt a connection in the first moment that we'd met, and we'd developed an informal, quasi mentor/mentee relationship of sorts. We'd often find a few minutes together when I was in the office for other meetings, and I loved how smart and earnest he was. He was hyper-observant; he noticed things that a lot of other people would miss. He asked great questions and had very insightful ideas and strong opinions on how to improve things in the business. In a way, he had become another set of eyes and ears for me in the company and gave me a perspective that Janice could not. And that's how he came to tell me what had happened that morning in his first close encounter with Valley Alley.

Jimmy did his best to push his concerns aside and tamp down the butterflies as he stepped into Alley's office.

Alley was squinting at one of the three computer monitors arrayed around his large, immaculately organized desk. He raised a finger in Jimmy's direction as if to say *gimme a minute*, so Jimmy stood, awkwardly, while he waited for Alley to finish what he was doing. He felt a small bead of sweat trickle slowly down the middle of his back. *Just heated up from my bike ride*, Jimmy assured himself as he slipped off his backpack and set it on the floor.

Alley punched a decisive finger on his keyboard and swiveled his chair around to face Jimmy.

"Sorry about that, Jimmy! Good morning to you!" said Alley with a big, sudden smile as he jumped to his feet, stepped around his desk, and reached his hand out to grasp Jimmy's. "Have you had your coffee yet? C'mon! I need another myself."

He all but pulled Jimmy with him through the door and down the hall to the elevator.

"The coffee's that way," said Jimmy, pointing behind them in the direction of the break room. He was still shocked by the surprising, enthusiastic energy emanating from this guy. This was not at all what he'd expected, and he was feeling a little thrown by it.

"I don't know what that is, but it's not coffee," laughed Alley. "Let's go get the real thing."

They jumped in Alley's rented Tesla and after a ten-minute drive filled with animated smalltalk about life in San Diego, they parked in a space across the street from the Wake-Up Call.

"Janice brought me here on my first visit to town during our courtship process. I became an instant regular. Ever been here?" asked Alley as he pulled the door open for Jimmy.

He hadn't. But Jimmy felt right at home as soon as they stepped through the doorway.

A few minutes later, seated and settled at a back corner table with a steaming mug of coffee in front of each of them, Jimmy reached for his backpack and started to pull a folder from its depths.

"I made copies of the spreadsheets for you," he began to say.

Alley held up his hand. "Hold on," he said. "Let's save that report for another time. I want to get your take on something else."

"Oh, okay. Sure," said Jimmy. "My take on what?"

In the moment, Jimmy told me later, he'd felt a pleasant jolt of pride that the COO wanted his opinion on something, whatever it was. But that nice feeling was tempered with a little intuitive voice of concern. It was like he saw a road sign in his mind that read *Caution: Ulterior Motive Ahead.*

"How's XinoniX treating you, Jimmy?"

"Treating me? I love it here," he said, a little nervous now.

"Mmm. First job out of college, right?"

"Right. But I worked during school."

"Where?"

Jimmy took a sip of his coffee. "Um . . . Starbucks."

"Good company," said Alley. "Finance job?"

"Barista," said Jimmy.

Alley chuckled. "Yeah, I figured that. I'm just playing with ya. It's a noble thing. The world could always use a better latte," he said with a pump of irony.

But then Alley's brow scrunched up, his face serious now.

"I have some concerns, Jimmy."

"About me?" Jimmy tried not to let his voice reveal the jumping frog in his throat.

"No, no. Not at all, Jimmy. On the contrary. I'm interested in your fresh perspective. You've worked closely with Janice from time to time, right?"

"Yes. A few times."

"Most recently, how did she seem to you?"

"What do you mean?"

"I don't know. You tell me. How did she seem?" he asked again.

"Janice is awesome," said Jimmy, sounding a little more defensive than he'd intended to.

Alley sat quietly, giving space for Jimmy to continue. The silence closed around him like an itchy wool blanket.

"Maybe she was a little—I don't know—distant?" said Jimmy, feeling compelled to fill the uncomfortable void in the conversation. When he heard himself say that out loud, Jimmy realized that it was truer than he'd cared to admit. Janice had been distant—absent, even. But instinctively, he felt it better to keep that to himself and not elaborate for Alley.

"Distant how?" pressed Alley.

"Why are you asking me this?" Jimmy said, finding the courage to voice his discomfort over this sudden line of interrogation.

"Okay, I'll level with you," said Alley, his eyes locked on Jimmy's. "I'm telling you this in absolute confidence, got it?"

"Okay," Jimmy said, hoping he didn't sound as reluctant as he felt.

"I think it's time to give this company a new focus, and I'm going to need help from the rank and file to get it done. I'd like to count on you for that help."

Jimmy felt the sweat on his back again, but this time it wasn't from a bike ride.

CHAPTER 10

Cat Cassidy's knuckles cracked as she interlaced her fingers and stretched her palms out in front of her. "Okay," she said, shaking her hands out as if getting ready to shred away on her guitar. "I'll share my own little technique with you, but keep in mind that this is something that works for me, and I'm not saying it'll work as well for you, Janice."

"Well, it has to be better than what I'm doing now," Janice scoffed at herself.

"The technical term for which is 'nothing,'" I said, feeling my attempt at ironic humor fall flat on its face in the middle of the table where we were all sitting.

Cat continued, unfazed by my rapier wit. "You know the old truism that *what gets measured gets done*, yes? Well, I start by devoting a week to measuring my own commitments and seeing how well I live up to them."

"I think I can devote a week to that," said Janice. "But that seems like a tricky thing to measure."

"Why?" asked Jim.

"Well, Farber and I have talked about this before." Janice looked at me.

"We have?" I raised my brows.

"Yes . . . you told me that sometimes people think I'm making a commitment when I don't even realize that I have—or I didn't intend to in the first place."

Yep. That sounded like something I'd say.

"Exactly!" said Cat. "And the key thing you just said was 'I don't even realize.' This process is all about *realizing*. In the moment. Being deeply self-aware of everything you say to others—right as you're saying them."

"Wow, that's a tall order, Cat," Janice mused.

"Yes, it is. But you do get better at it. And remember, it's only for a week. And during that week, you're going to pay very close attention to your own words and challenge yourself to treat your every utterance as though you've just signed a contract. I call it *speaking with a contractual attitude*. See what that intention does to your thought process, and, even more important, your actions."

Cat paused to let that sink in. "So," she continued after a moment, "do you want to know the process? No commitment until you hear the whole thing." Cat smiled reassuringly.

"Yes," we all exclaimed in near-unison.

Looked like Janice wasn't the only one at the table who needed a little help in this regard. To capture Cat's guidelines as she spelled them out for us, I fished my ever-ready journaling notepad out of my briefcase. (I call it a WUP, or

Wake-Up Pad—something I learned about many years ago while having a discussion with a friend at the Wake-Up Call diner, hence the name.)

"First of all," Cat began. "Make sure you have a notebook—like Steve's, for example—or a device of some kind that you can easily use in the moment and keep it with you at all times during your Contractual Attitude Week."

"That has a nice ring to it, but *CAW* doesn't make for the greatest acronym," I mused aloud as I considered the words I'd just written on the page. "I muse aloud too much, don't I?" I said to the group in my inimitable, self-deprecating style.

"Hold that thought," Cat smiled. "We're coming to that in a minute."

In the next few minutes, Cat enumerated her process, which I captured in my WUP as she talked us through it.

"Number one," Cat began, "each day, write down every overt or obvious promise or commitment you make. In other words, when you explicitly say you're going to do something, capture it in writing—like a contract—right there and then. For example, let's say that Barry and I are having a chat about something, and we get off on a tangent about our favorite snacks. I mention that I make killer chocolate chunk cookies and bring them to the office on special occasions. Turns out that Barry loves chocolate chunk cookies, so I offer to send him my recipe. And he is, of course, ecstatic about that."

"Obviously!" laughed Barry.

"So what would I do in that moment, Barry?" asked Cat, acting the professor with the professor.

"Write it down," he said.

"Yup! I'm going to write *send cookie recipe to Barry Posner* in my contract journal. See? Simple, right? So be on the lookout for overt commitments you're making to your coworkers and clients, to your friends and family, and—and this may be the hardest of all—to yourself. Write. Them. All. Down. At the end of the day, you're going to find that you've made a ton of commitments to lots of different people, and you will have a most impressive list of contractual items."

"Geez," said Janice, rubbing her forehead. She was obviously chagrined at the prospect of overwhelm.

"I know . . . it feels like a lot," said Cat. "But guess what?"

We all looked at her.

"That's the easy part," she said to us with a wry smile. "The next one is where it gets really challenging." She paused for dramatic effect.

"Number two, write down every *implied* promise or commitment you make. To do that, you have to be hyperaware of the casual, thinking-out-loud things you say that could be interpreted by the listener as a commitment—*musing aloud*, as Steve called it a minute ago. The more important you are to someone, the higher the regard they hold for you, the more likely they are to take what you're saying as a promise. And as CEOs, Janice, we are automatically held in the highest regard by just about everyone who works with us.

"For example," Cat continued. "Let's say you work in my company. We'll call you Billy Bob."

"Alrighty," I said, with what I felt was a stereotypically appropriate drawl.

"And you know I'm a pretty good guitar player."

"Yeah. Pretty good," I laughed, acknowledging her trademark humility.

"One day, we're talking in my office," said Cat. "And you happen to tell me that you're a keyboard player. *Awesome!* I say. *You should come jam with us sometime.* I said it because it's a polite thing to say, and maybe I meant it in the moment. But then—poof—it's gone from my memory and, as far as I'm concerned, that's the end of that. But what did you, the eager, excited, piano-playing employee, hear? *I'm going to jam with Cat!* And then you tell all your co-worker friends about it. And then you wait for the invitation from me. And it never comes. So you're deeply disappointed, and your friends keep asking you about it, so you're embarrassed, and you finally tell them that Cat didn't follow through after all. *I guess she was just blowing smoke*, you say. My credibility takes a hit with you and, by extension, with your colleagues, too. And I am completely unaware that this is going on. Now, in my defense, it's not because I was lying to you, but I just wasn't cognizant of the impact of my words in that moment.

"But if I were holding myself to the standard of speaking with a contractual attitude, and I was, therefore, self-aware in the moment, I either wouldn't have said those words at all, or

I would have written it down in my contract journal: *send Billy Bob an invitation to jam next Thursday*. Because as soon as those words came out of my mouth, they became a commitment that demands my follow-through."

I felt a sinking feeling in my stomach. And it wasn't from the beer.

"Yow," I said. "I think I do that way too much."

"Yes, you do, Steve," said Cat.

I winced; she wasn't going to let me off the hook, was she?

"And I know that because we all do," she said making eye contact with each of us in turn. "It's our collective, unconscious habit. Maybe it's because we're inclined to be accommodating. Or maybe we just want to say something that makes the other person feel good, or connected, or valued by us in the moment. Whatever the reasons, we make unintended, implied commitments a lot, and that's why developing a contractual attitude demands focus and practice.

"Which brings us to number three. At the end of each day, you have a growing list of both intentional and implied contract items. What are you going to do with those?"

"Give them to an assistant?" I asked. I can't help myself.

Cat ignored me, of course. "You're going to start scoring yourself. Put a checkmark next to each thing you followed through on and tally them up. And roll over the pending items to the next day. Rinse and repeat for the entire week. And then—and this is number four—at the end of the week, you're going to quantitatively assess your performance: How many promises did you keep? How many did you either forget about or consciously blow off?"

"What gets measured gets done," Janice recited.

"That's the idea," said Cat. "But it's also important to reflect on your experience.

"So number five is just that: reflect. How did you feel during the week? What did you learn about yourself and others? Where did you stumble and why? Do you see any patterns in the commitments you followed through on and the ones you didn't? Where did you excel? And lots of other questions along those lines. And it's a good idea to journal your thoughts on this and see how it evolves over time."

"There's a lot of self-discovery in that journey," said Jim. He hadn't said anything for some time, I realized. He'd been giving Cat's words and ideas a lot of thought. "I bet it'll bring out some personal insights that'll last a lifetime. I'm in; I'm going to do it. How about you, Janice?"

"How can I say no?" she smiled at Jim. "But only for a week, right?"

"Um . . . sure," said Cat. "Only for a week. And then see if you want to go again. You may surprise yourself, Janice."

Spontaneously, we all clinked our glasses together over the middle of the table, each agreeing to jump on board for the next week.

"Thank you so much, Cat," Janice said quietly. "I really needed this."

Prophetic words, indeed.

She would soon see how much of an understatement that was.

CHAPTER 11

Lessons learned, new friendships forged, and myriad selfies snapped all added up to an evening to remember. That was one for the scrapbooks, to be sure. I know that I, at least, had ridden a wave of inspiration over the month since we'd all gone our separate ways that night. Maybe I had let something slip here and there, but for two full weeks, I was otherwise meticulous with my contract journal. My follow-through score was trending up, but most significant was how much more aware of my own words I'd become. Not only was I getting better at living up to my spoken promises, but I was frequently catching myself and keeping my mouth shut instead of musing out loud about things that I wasn't likely to act on. The journal was just a tool, I now saw, for creating a new habit of adopting the so-called contractual attitude. I really felt like I was getting the hang of it.

Janice and I hadn't spoken in at least a few weeks, so I was curious how she was doing with her own DWYSYWD endeavors at XinoniX. I jotted down a reminder to give her a shout later that evening, and just as I'd jotted the last jot, my phone lit up with a text from the woman herself.

"SOS," it said, simply. Man, those three little letters are powerful motivators.

A few minutes later, I poked the screen in my car to return her call as I drove from the airport up to my house in northern San Diego County. Poway, a suburban town with the quaint tagline "The City in the Country," had been my home for several years since Nikki and I had gotten hitched and started the next chapter of our lives together. It was a thirty-minute drive from the airport, so I knew the trip should give me ample time to hear from Janice and talk her off whatever ledge my twisted imagination was conjuring up for her in this moment. Whatever the reality was, I knew it couldn't be good. In the two decades I'd known her, Janice had never sent me a literal SOS. And I mean never.

In a hushed voice, she spoke quickly and with a tone of urgency, both of which she tended to do when she was under pressure. When I'm under pressure, I nap. We're a good balance that way.

She started with an admission of guilt, which never bodes well for any situation. Even with all her best intentions, Janice told me, she hadn't been keeping her journal or—even more important—spending as much time in the office as she'd planned on.

"You mean, committed to," I interjected, and immediately regretted saying out loud. This wasn't a time to poke a finger in the wound—as if there ever was.

"I know, I *know*," she said, breathless. "We had a couple of upcoming big fundraising events for the nonprofit, which, by the way, I had already committed to running. And then a big donor backed out at the last minute, so I had to put that fire out and find a way to fill the funding gap, and then it was one more thing after another. I just got overrun with that responsibility, but I knew that it would be temporary. So I kept telling myself that all I had to do was get these few philanthropic things out of the way, and then I could refocus at XinoniX. And I did. That's all done now, so I'm back. For good. And I mean it. But . . ."

She railed on, describing how, in her absence, Alley had enlisted several members of the board and a cadre of influential XinoniX employees to—in her characterization—undermine her influence and minimize her contribution to the company's success. She felt that Alley was trying to create a case for removing Janice from the CEO position, which would mean, of course, forcing her out of the enterprise altogether.

Once he had established a base of support, Janice told me, Alley started holding town hall meetings with the whole company where he took questions from employees, gave updates on financials, and bantered about the latest industry news—all good stuff, of course. But those were all the things that Janice had traditionally done. And he hadn't been holding these meetings as Janice's representative, or even as her teammate. It had been "*The Alley Show*," and he was clearly enjoying the attention.

"And you know what's even worse?" Janice said. "He hasn't mentioned our LEAP values once. Not even once."

I could feel the hurt in her voice. It had been a long-standing tradition at XinoniX—since the days the company was founded by Teddy Garrison, in fact—to start every meeting with a round of accolades for and stories about people who had cultivated Love, generated Energy, inspired Audacity, and provided Proof in authentic and tangible ways in the business. Janice had been the torch-bearer of those founding principles since she'd first joined the company as a junior member of the marketing team. And she'd sworn to uphold those values when Teddy had passed the role to her.

I wasn't surprised that Janice felt so deeply about all this, and I knew why she was so distressed by LEAP's sudden absence at the hands of the COO. Yes, this was personal to her. But it went way beyond sentiment; it was also about operational excellence.

Not only were those values prominently displayed on the walls of the company headquarters, the website, their marketing collateral, and all employees' email signatures, but even more important, they hired, fired, and gave ownership based on adherence to those values. They had worked hard to weave them into their performance appraisals, so expectations associated with each value were clearly understood by everyone, and everyone was rewarded (or not) based on adherence to those expectations.

And it was one of the first things I'd learned about the company back when I first met them a couple of decades before. In fact, I had been so impressed with the work they'd done, I kept their performance evaluations in a special file in my desk and had referred to them many times over the years as a fine example of a values-based appraisal.

The item on Proof, for example, read as follows (rated on a scale of 1 to 5, where 1 = Unacceptable, 2 = Passable, 3 = On Par, 4 = Strong, 5 = Extraordinary):

PROVIDING PROOF: Proving love of XinoniX and commitment to colleagues, contractors, and clients through measurable results.

1. *Performs tasks and gets things done primarily out of a desire for completion; doesn't tie daily tasks and contributions to a greater commitment to and love of colleagues, contractors, and clients.*
2. *Generates measurable results and, to some extent, ties daily tasks and contributions to a greater commitment to and love of colleagues, contractors, and clients. Looks for opportunities to fulfill the XinoniX business objectives and provide feedback to improve those objectives.*
3. *Seeks to provide unequivocal proof that supports the values of Extreme Leadership & XinoniX in everything they do. Is intolerant of behavior inconsistent with our values and is prepared to be heard.*

4. *Proves commitment to and love of colleagues, contractors, and clients through strong performance results. Is a key contributor to creating the goals, values, and objectives of their department and through own actions, causes those goals, values, and objectives to be realized.*
5. *Consistently and powerfully proves commitment to and love of colleagues, contractors, and clients through exceptionally strong results. Performs every deed as though their every action has a direct impact on our brand and the world of our colleagues, contractors, and clients. Willing to make personal sacrifice to prove their love.*

So it was easy to see why Janice took Alley's ignoring of LEAP not so much as a personal affront, but as a broadside attack on the culture of the company she loved so dearly.

"And it goes on," she said as I pulled into my driveway. "I'll tell you more later, but I need your help with something right away."

Here's the thing: I'd already heard everything she'd just told me. My friend Jimmy had been giving me frequent reports from the field, as it were. He, too, was distressed by what he saw happening around him at the company, but he was also kind of enjoying playing intelligence officer. Alley believed that Jimmy was one of the folks in his corner. Not that Jimmy lied about it, more like he let Alley believe what he wanted to. And I had agreed to keep my mouth shut with Janice until Jimmy had had a chance to connect with her and share his concerns directly.

All of which I now confessed to Janice.

"Okay," she said. "I'm not surprised. But that's not what my SOS is about."

I powered down my car. "Alright then," I said. "What's going on?"

"The board has summoned me to a meeting tomorrow morning, and I'd like you to come with me."

"Sure," I said, not feeling quite as confident as I sounded. "What's the plan?"

"More than anything, I'll need your moral support."

"Sure," I repeated. "But what's the plan?"

"I need to get rid of Alley," she said.

It's amazing how fast the mind works. For the last few seconds, it was like my brain had jumped into a time machine in the form of a red-hot Ferrari, blazed down to the end of memory lane, pulled a screeching 180, and smoked its way back to the present moment to join me here in the XinoniX conference room with Janice, Alley, and the assembled members of the board.

"Janice," Alley was saying calmly. "The board is in agreement that the time has come for you and XinoniX to part ways."

CHAPTER 12

Bob Jeffers finished his early morning powerwalk through the Palm Springs neighborhood he had retired to after leaving XinoniX. He threw his proprietary concoction of powders and proteins into the Vitamix, tossed in a few ice cubes, and cranked it to eleven. Still old school in some respects, Bob liked to read actual newspapers every morning while savoring his smoothie. When taken together, he figured *The Wall Street Journal* and *The New York Times* gave him a more or less balanced view of the state of the social landscape. And to keep him connected to his roots, the *San Diego Business Journal* rounded out his information trinity. He tucked the three papers under his arm and stepped outside to the patio table to take it all in alfresco.

On that particular morning, the day he retrieved the weekly San Diego publication from his mailbox, he picked up the *Business Journal* first and scanned the pages until one particularly disturbing headline jumped off the page and grabbed him by the eyeballs.

Local Biotech XinoniX Announces Alastair Langstrom as New COO

When he'd retired as the company's CEO, Bob had promised himself that he would leave XinoniX behind and let it live peacefully and fondly in his memory. He loved the company, and he had no doubt that Janice would continue to do a stellar job as its custodian, so other than an occasional wisp of nostalgia, he felt no pull, no vestigial attachment to his past.

But this article made him realize that he still had a strong, visceral connection to the company and to Janice that went far beyond sentimental memories. He was alarmed at what he'd read and he felt an urgent need to react—something he hadn't experienced since the day he'd retired. He had encountered Alastair Langstrom on a couple of occasions at various tech functions in recent years. The guy had charm, and he seemed to be well liked by most folks, but from the very first time they'd met, something about Valley Alley made Bob feel—and this is a technical term—icky. So, mostly out of curiosity, he'd asked around.

From his working days and through his membership and leadership experience in several influential industry trade associations, Bob had personal relationships with a whole slew of Silicon Valley executives and power players. He took advantage of the fact that he had many of those folks on speed dial. And dial he did.

That's when he heard the stories of the manifold bruised and broken bodies Alley had apparently left in his professional wake. He had a rep of serving his own ambitions at the expense of the people around him. Oh sure, he got results. But the real issue was about how he got them. He was a masterful corporate politician quite adept at deflecting blame for setbacks and taking credit for accomplishments. "You can't trust him," were the words Bob had heard again and again.

And those were the same words he had texted me that very morning: *Read that Langstrom is new COO. You can't trust him.*

As soon as he'd hit the send button on that rather potent message, he'd felt immediate regret for meddling in something that was literally no longer his business. So he'd just set his phone aside, tried to forget that he'd ever reacted, and did his best to pretend that his words would have no real impact.

And he did a pretty good job of putting it out of his mind. Until he got a call from me some time later, on that fateful day when Janice got canned.

CHAPTER 13

Years back, Janice had purchased a tri-level in Mission Beach, which turned out to be quite the astute investment—especially after the COVID-era real estate pricing spike in San Diego County. It sat right on Mission Bay, just a few short blocks to the east from the ocean and its famed boardwalk. The building had three separate living spaces: a ground-floor apartment, which Janice rented out to a long-time friend; a beautiful second-floor apartment, which she used as her home office and guest accommodations; and the third-floor unit, which gave Janice lots of privacy and rooftop access, was the place she called home.

I loved this neighborhood. And this particular building held a lot of fond memories for me. Every time I visited, I was flooded with a nostalgic wave of feelings for and images of people I'd met and lessons I'd learned. Because once upon a time, you see, that second-story flat had been mine. And it was there, a couple of decades earlier, from that very cool pad in Mission Beach, where I'd first learned about Extreme Leadership and The Radical Leap.

Her rooftop deck afforded a sweeping view of the Pacific Ocean, and Janice found herself spending more time up there in recent months. It gave her an inspiring place to reflect and recharge. It was also the ideal turf to pace, back and forth and over and over, while she tried to sort things out. Janice paced when things got stressful, and after yesterday's bombshell board meeting, she was now in full-on Ludicrous Mode, as the Tesla folks like to say.

I sat and watched her back-and-forth like a spectator at the San Diego Open. Aside from an occasional mumble, Janice was silent. As was I. I knew she was still reeling after being let go in a majority decision by the XinoniX board, and I was fully aware that I was witnessing her descent into the proverbial dark night of the soul. And—in this moment, anyway—I felt that my quiet presence was the best way to support her.

A fresh ocean breeze blew across the deck, and the juxtaposition of this beautiful sunny day with Janice's midnight funk was not lost on either of us, I suspect.

"He should be here any minute," I said, breaking the silence.

"Okay," said Janice, forcing a smile. "I left the front door unlocked."

"Cool," I said.

"It'll be good to see him."

"Yes, it will," I agreed with a smile that I hoped would feel reassuring to her.

Janice stopped her striding and stepped over near me. The two of us stood side by side and gazed in resumed silence over the sparkling water of the bay as we waited for him to arrive.

A few minutes later, he stepped through the rooftop door and called out to us. Janice and I turned, and she all but raced over to hug him. I was taken aback at the enthusiasm of her embrace, which struck me as being affectionate, but also a little bit . . . what? Desperate, maybe? She held him close and didn't let go.

His hair was white and wispy, and as he smiled at me over Janice's shoulder, I noticed that the age spots on his tan face were more prominent than the last time we'd been together. His blue eyes caught the sunlight, and they shone with a serenity that I'd never noticed in him before. He looked lean and fit—a testament, I figured, to his ritual of powerwalking in the early morning desert air. Retirement had been good to Bob Jeffers.

Janice released Bob from her grasp. When she turned, I saw the tears running down her face, which she hastily wiped away with the heel of her hand.

"I'm sorry," she said. "I'm just so happy to see you."

"Oh c'mon, kid," said Bob. "What are you apologizing for? You know how much I love tears," he laughed. He might have meant that as gentle sarcasm, but it didn't seem that way to me.

I'd known Janice for a long time, and we'd seen each other go through some tough stuff over the years. But I couldn't recall any instance where she'd been as vulnerable with me as she was with Bob in that moment. I now saw that there was a tenderness between them that I'd never been aware of before, and I felt instantly reassured—and a little proud of myself—that I'd had the instinct to suggest to Bob that he make the trip to San Diego to spend some time with Janice in her moment of personal crisis.

"Come," said Bob, putting his hands on Janice's shoulders and guiding her toward a nearby table. He shot me a quick tilt of the head to indicate that I should follow along and join the two of them.

"So," he said to Janice, gently, "tell me."

And that was all the prompting she needed. She started at the beginning of the Alley story and brought him right up to the previous day when, in a four-to-two decision, the board had elected to unceremoniously cast her out.

"On what basis?" Bob asked.

"They said I had been shirking my obligations as CEO by focusing too much of my time elsewhere, and they used a recent quarter of mild underexpected results as the justification. But the real issue wasn't any of that."

"Alley?" said Bob.

"Of course. Alley. In retrospect, I can see that he was gunning for my job from the minute he walked in the door. He found sympathetic people on the board and cozied up to them, convincing them that he would be their golden ticket. And he persistently built his case, by cherry-picking numbers, stories, and events to shore up his cause. At least, that's what I suspect."

"And here we are," I said. I wanted Janice to let go of what had transpired and to begin focusing on her path forward. "So where do you want to go from here?"

"Before you answer that," Bob said, putting his hand on my arm as if to say *let me take the reins for a bit,* "there's something I'd like you to think about."

"Good. Because I have absolutely no idea where to go from here," she said, answering my question with a forced smile. "Truth is, I'm crushed. I feel like my core has been ripped out of me by a red-haired, rabid weasel. I feel betrayed. Lost. And so, so . . . sad." She wiped fresh tears away with the back of her hand.

"Like your center of gravity is gone?" asked Bob.

"Yes. Like that."

"Well," Bob smiled. "It's not; it's still there. You just have to remember your way back to it."

Janice breathed in deeply and let out a rush of air through pursed lips.

Bob chuckled. "Good. Take a few more of those breaths and then we'll try something."

She did, and I found myself reflexively breathing along.

"Do you have a dictation app on your phone?" He pointed to her ever-present device. Janice nodded and started swiping through her screen.

"Got it," she said.

"Good. Open that up and get ready to record." He paused and gave her time to comply. "Ready?"

"I don't know," said Janice, warily. "What am I recording?"

"First, I'd like you to look back and take stock of everything you've learned from your personal and professional experiences so far. The good in your life, and the bad; the beautiful and the ugly; the complex and the mundane. I'm not asking you to remember every detail, and I don't want to hear your autobiography—just let the memories and the feelings of your experiences wash over you for a moment."

We all sat in silence for a few minutes, and I found myself awash in my own memories as well. It's astonishing how fast our brains can access and recall the particulars of our journeys. I guess you don't have to wait for your final moments on this planet to have your life flash before your eyes; you can call it up any time you want.

"Good? Now hit record."

She did.

"Okay," Bob continued. "Now complete this sentence: *As a leader, I believe . . .*"

Janice waited.

"And?"

"And that's it. Complete that sentence."

"Okay, okay. Got it. As a leader, I believe . . ." her words trailed off as she grasped for the words. "I believe that every person has value."

"Good," said Bob. "Now, again: I believe . . ."

"I believe that every person has value," Janice repeated.

Bob laughed. "No—it's not a mantra. What *else* do you believe? *I believe . . .*" he prompted her again.

"I believe that we can accomplish anything together."

"Great. Keep going."

"I believe that Alley is a manipulative ass hat."

"Hah!" I exclaimed, in spite of myself. I truly loved Janice's irreverent streak. Not because it reminded me of myself or anything.

"Did you get that out of your system?" asked Bob, amused in spite of himself. "Good. Go on."

Janice took another deep breath.

"I believe that we should always be honest with each other."

Now she was on a roll.

"I believe that love is the highest standard. I believe that our job is to change the world for the better. I believe that we should always strive for excellence. I believe that we should do what we love in the service of people who love what we do. I believe that as long as we cultivate love, generate energy, inspire audacity, and provide proof, we'll stay true to our cause. And when we hit roadblocks, I believe that challenge is always the opportunity for greatness."

"What kind of challenges?" Bob interjected.

"Any kind of challenge," she answered without hesitation.

"How about the challenge of being unexpectedly and unceremoniously canned by an ungrateful board?" I asked, picking up on where Bob was going with that last question.

"So you're saying that my situation is an opportunity for greatness."

"No. That's what you said, Janice," I said.

"Yeah. Well, it's a little hard to see that right now." Her eyes misted again.

"Just because it's hard to see," said Bob softly, "doesn't make it any less true, does it?"

Bob asked Janice to take a few minutes and silently read back over her app's transcription of her list of "I believes."

And while she did, I closed my eyes and listened to the sound of the ocean waves rumbling in the distance—which they always do, no matter what joys or trepidations we're experiencing in our lives. I always found comfort in that.

"That feels comforting," said Janice, as if reading my sea-inspired thoughts. She set her phone in her lap. "It's a good reminder of what's really important."

"And that reminder is going to be of *utmost* importance for a while," said Bob, standing and stretching his legs.

"Have you communicated with any of the XinoniX team yet? Have you reached out to anyone to let them know what happened?" he asked.

"My lawyer says I shouldn't—at least not for now."

"Got it. Makes sense," said Bob. "Okay, here's what I'd like you to do. I'd like for you to write a letter—a memo of sorts—to the XinoniX employees. You'll send it later, when the time is right, but write it now, while these thoughts are fresh."

Janice looked puzzled. "What thoughts?"

"That list of the principles you believe in. Use those, and turn them into a note that says, in essence, *These are the things I'd like you to remember and strive to live by in my absence*—which may well be forever."

"A Credo Memo," I said, smiling.

"Yes. Exactly," Bob replied. "It's a classic Kouzes and Posner process, as you know." He raised his eyebrows in acknowledgment.

"The word 'credo' means 'I believe,'" I said to Janice. "So Bob is asking you to write a memorandum of your beliefs—your credo—to leave with your team."

"Right now?"

"Yes," Bob answered. "Write it right now. Steve and I will leave you to it while we take a little stroll on the beach.

We don't have any of that in the desert, you know. Or, rather, it's all beach and no ocean."

Janice had her instructions, and Bob and I headed down the stairs, out of her house, and over to the boardwalk that ran along the beach.

We walked along in silence for a few minutes as we sucked in the invigorating Pacific Ocean air. The quiet didn't last very long, as I was bursting with curiosity to ask him a question.

"Bob? A Credo Memo? Do you know Jim and Barry?" I exclaimed. That would have been just too much of a coincidence for my wee brain to handle.

"Well, no. Not personally. But I've read a few of their books, and I've always loved the Credo Memo idea. I never wrote one myself, and since I retired, I've often felt regret that I hadn't. At the very least, it would have been so cool to have done that when I first left. So . . . I guess this is my vicarious opportunity through Janice."

"You know that those guys are my mentors, right?"

He hadn't. So, as we took our short constitutional on the boardwalk, I told Bob about Janice's introduction to and encounter with Jim and Barry, and how they'd been so gracious and generous with their time and wisdom with our mutual friend and colleague. I had fun watching Bob's face and seeing his eyebrows raise repeatedly in surprise and delight about the seeming coincidence of it all.

We returned to the rooftop from our pleasant walk-and-talk and found Janice pacing—as usual—and looking at her legal pad as she moved hither and yon across the deck. She motioned for us to join her.

"Okay," she said, hugging her pad close to her chest. "I was picturing the whole team huddled together in the office lobby while someone—not sure who yet—would read this message to everyone on my behalf."

"Cool," I said, picturing the dramatic scene. "And where is Alley in this scenario?"

"Oh, I imagine he's off somewhere taking a flying f—"

"Okay, okay, we got it," laughed Bob, cutting her off before she went astray on an unproductive rant. "Let's hear it."

"And I really felt the team there," she continued, ignoring Bob's instruction. "And, the thing is, I really, really miss them. I miss having a community. I miss my friends, and I . . ." her voice trailed off. She was obviously distraught. Bob and I waited in silence for her to collect her thoughts.

After a few minutes, Janice turned her pad around to show us her work. The page was blank.

"I tried," she said. "I really did."

Her voice quavered as she looked out at the horizon of the ocean. "I just can't do this right now. Can you guys give me a little time? I feel like I just need to step back for a bit."

"Of course," Bob and I said, almost in unison.

"I keep thinking about what Cat said to me that evening," Janice said to me. "Whenever she's faced with a challenge, her first response is always to check to see if she still believes in herself and in the values she'd subscribed to. I think that's what I need to figure out for myself. I've clearly let people down, and I've let myself down. And Alley moved in to take advantage of my not showing up the way I should have. And he shouldn't have done that.

He should have helped me, not betrayed my trust. But I can't deny that I gave him the opening, and I have to figure out why I wasn't acting in accordance with all of those beliefs I just told you about. Do I really believe those things like I once did? And if so, am I still capable of living up to them?"

"Take whatever time you need," said Bob after a few silent moments. "I'm happy to hang around for a couple of days, if you'd like to meet again later this week."

"Thank you," said Janice with a sad smile. "But I'm going to get away for a while."

"What? Where?" I asked, surprised at this turn of events.

She shook her head slowly. "Not sure exactly. Don't know where I'm going, but I know what I need to do once I get there."

"What's that?" I asked.

Janice looked out over the Pacific Ocean as the sun slowly descended to the horizon. She absentmindedly scratched at a newly forming patch of redness on her arm.

"Heal," she said.

CHAPTER 14

"Hey, Steve," the recording began. "I'm going to give you the play-by-play of what happened today in Alley's first town hall meeting since Janice's departure."

Jimmy Sun's voice piped into my ear through my AirPods. To keep me updated on the goings-on at the company, Jimmy had been sending me the occasional text notes, but this was the first time he'd done a full-on recording.

"I figure that speaking this out will be a lot faster than having to write grammatically correct sentences for you." That was a little dig at my persnickety attention to the proper usage of our oft-mangled language. I mean, *really*. A grown-up person should know the difference between "your" and "you're" and "they're" and "their" and "its" and "it's," right? I even proofread my texts before I send them. Yes, it takes a little more time, but I figure if some intel officer in China is monitoring everything I'm writing, I'm going to be sure I'm making the right impression. Consider it my small contribution to global détente.

Jimmy continued with his narrative of the very meeting that Janice had heard about through the grapevine.

Alley had scheduled the town hall meeting precisely one week from the day Janice had been canned, and folks were relieved that he had apparently chosen to uphold the cherished company tradition. The town halls were a monthly opportunity for the entire company to gather and share stories of inspiration, celebrate recent accomplishments, and talk to the leadership about issues, suggestions, and, of course, complaints. Month after month and year after year—even during the pandemic when everything had switched to Zoom—people from all levels and functions looked forward to the collective energy of their traditional gathering.

There'd been a lot of speculation as to how this meeting was going to go, Jimmy told me. On the one hand, everyone was looking forward to it, as they always had; on the other, they expected it to feel different with Janice gone and Alley officially in charge, but in what way, no one knew for sure. So the mood in the room was tense, and the gathered participants were jittery.

I'd like to think that Alley had been nervous in anticipation of his first public showing as the company's CEO, but I guess I'll never know. By all appearances, though, he was cool as a sea cucumber as he wound his way to the front of the main room of the company's cafeteria.

He hooked in his laptop and fired up the projector to reveal a PowerPoint slide with several graphs and text typed in a font so tiny that it looked like ants squished on the screen. He tapped his microphone a couple of times and asked for everyone's attention.

"Good morning," said Alley. "Let's dive right in and look at the latest performance data."

A hand shot up from the back of the room.

"Excuse me!" she called out, which seemed to startle Alley a bit. "I know you've done a few meetings while Janice was still CEO, and I don't know if anyone's told you before, but we're supposed to do numbers later. Janice always starts with the latest LEAP stories, and then we do recognition and stuff like that."

"Tell me your name, please," Alley said, after a pause.

"Sondra."

"And how long have you been here?" he asked.

"Twenty-five years," she said, her words sparking an enthusiastic round of applause from her colleagues.

"I thank you for your service," said Alley, apparently trying to get a laugh with the military reference. Pardon the pun here, but it bombed. An uneasy silence permeated the room.

"Listen, Sandra . . ."

"Sondra," she corrected.

"Sorry . . . Sondra," he said. "I know that change can be difficult, but going forward, we'll be shifting our focus as a company. I'm not saying that company values don't have value; I've written quite a few mission statements in my career. But the time you all take talking about LEAP and telling stories and all that is time much better spent focusing on our objectives and KPIs."

Sondra had a reputation, mostly a good one, for speaking her mind. And today was no exception.

"Okay, but you do realize that we've been a very successful company, right?" she said, standing now. "We've made great money, won awards, and stuff like that. So we've clearly been doing something good, right? And we're proud of the work we've done, right?" She directed that last comment to her colleagues, clearly looking for support. Many heads nodded, but there was no applause.

"I'll be blunt," said Alley to everyone, as Sondra sat down. "The company's been coasting lately. And if you don't know that, you haven't been paying attention. Don't you think you can do better?" he challenged, moving his gaze across the room.

"Well, I sure hope you do. Because if any of you are planning on just cruising along, there's no place for you here. We are going to set records. We're gonna kill it. 'Something good' is not good enough anymore.".

The red on his face was beginning to match the color of his hair.

"You need to know this about me: I have a track record of getting results; I'm known for it. Google me. I know how to get it done. And the way we're going to get things done around here will be to put our collective attention and effort where it belongs: on the numbers.

"Has anyone ever heard the phrase 'What gets measured gets done?'"

Several hands went up, but not enthusiastically.

"Well, we're going to measure the hell out of our performance metrics in all areas, and we're going to get them done. And we're going to be transparent with those numbers, too. You'll all see them, and you'll all be held accountable to them. Whether you *love* it or not," he'd added with a sneer.

Sondra, who was sitting next to Jimmy, turned to him and whispered.

"Well," she said, barely containing her frustration. "It was good while it lasted—for two and a half freaking decades."

Alley turned his attention to the glowing screen behind him.

"Now," he continued, squinting at the slide with his back to the audience. "If there are no other questions, let's take a look at next quarter's objectives."

There were no other questions.

CHAPTER 15

Over the next six months, Alley was determined to re-create XinoniX in his own image and, when it came to anything LEAP related, he went into full-on deconstruction mode. First, the old values statement disappeared from the company website, then the "Do What You Love in the Service of People Who Love What You Do" quote that had been inscribed on the reception-area wall was covered over with a fresh coat of paint. More significant, though, was his announcement that the performance evaluation process was under review and would be revised to reflect the new priorities and company KPIs.

Jimmy was so distraught, he told me, he was putting his résumé together—something that he never thought he would have to do. At least not by choice.

I was watching all of this from a distance and mostly through Jimmy's eyes—although I heard similar things from other folks through the ranks, and, despite my

characteristically chill constitution, I was feeling the frustration build in my chest anytime I thought about it. And the fact that Janice was still absent and radio-silent didn't help my frame of mind much, either.

And on top of all that, rumor had it that the company's numbers were on a sharp uptick in these early days of Alley's reign, which he used as further justification and positive evidence for the changes he was making.

One afternoon, finding myself in a deeper-than-usual funk, I felt inspired to reach out to Jim and Barry to request a Zoom get-together, which we quickly arranged for the following week.

It uplifted my spirits to see their faces, albeit in a virtual room, and we started right in to the usual banter and good-natured teasing.

Once we got that out of our systems, I filled them in on everything that I knew about the current situation with XinoniX, Alley, Janice, and the whole gut-wrenching scenario unfolding in the San Diego HQ.

"I told Jimmy that I would reach out to Alley, just to see if he'd be willing to have a chat. I did have a pretty good rapport with him until all of this broke loose."

"So, what did Alley say when you messaged him?" asked Barry.

"Yes! I'm so curious," Jim added. "That's a pretty bold request, all things considered."

"Well, I haven't done it," I said. "And I'm not sure I'm going to. It feels really awkward, and I don't know how appropriate it is, if I'm being honest."

"Mmm-hmm," said Barry with a half-smile curving up under his mustache.

"Well, are you?" asked Jim.

"Am I what?"

"Being honest. You said, 'If I'm being honest.' So, are you? Being honest?"

"Uh. Well. Yes, sure. I'm being honest. It does feel uncomfortable to reach out to Alley."

"But you told Jimmy you were going to," Jim persisted.

Uh-oh. I saw where this was going. "Yes, I did," I said slowly and probably a little too carefully.

"Did it feel uncomfortable in the moment? When you'd made that commitment to Jimmy?" Barry piled on.

"Umm, yes. It did, I guess. But first off, I don't know that I'd call it a commitment, and now that I've had some time to think about it, I . . ."

"Wait," said Barry, holding up his hand on the screen. "I want to read you something . . ." He clicked at the keys on his laptop. "Ah. Here it is."

He cleared his throat in dramatic fashion and began to read.

I embrace the reality that doing what you say you will do is not just important, it is imperative; therefore, I make a Radical Promise to hold myself 100% accountable to my own words. DWYSYWD is not a platitude. It's not a truism. It's a deep, soul-based commitment to the authentic core of who I am. All of this requires a significantly heightened sense of self-awareness, where I truly think before I speak. And once I speak, I know that it is not acceptable to retract. Having said that, I acknowledge that I am not perfect—no one is. I recognize that this is an impossible standard to live up to in an absolute and literal sense. But it is a truly significant, monumental aspiration to have for myself, because in the striving to live up to it, I create a much higher rate of consistency between my words and my actions. And that's all I can ask of myself as a fallible human being. Once I have established that standard for myself, it gives me the credibility to ask the same of others—which I fully intend to do.

"Sound familiar?" Barry concluded.

"Oh, shit," I said, ever the self-aware one.

"You have to ask yourself," said Jim, "if being 'uncomfortable' absolves you of the responsibility to be accountable to your own words—and to Jimmy's expectations of what you said you would do."

"No, it does not," I said, stating what now appeared to be so freakin' obvious. "I clearly was not speaking with a contractual attitude."

"Well, I think that's the right answer. Don't you, Barry?" asked Jim across the electrons of the virtual room.

"Well, now, that depends," said Barry, in response.

"On what?" asked Jim, fully knowing the answer.

"On what he does next," replied Barry, as if I weren't there.

And in a way, I wasn't. I had already picked up my phone and was lost in crafting just the right words in my text to Alley, requesting an audience with His Majesty.

I was going to need to make an attitude adjustment if this was going to work.

CHAPTER 16

As I rode up the elevator to Alley's floor in the XinoniX building, I breathed slowly to settle my racing heartbeat (in through the nose . . . and . . . out through the mouth . . . two . . . three . . . four). Surprised that he had agreed to a short sit-down—*I can give you 20 minutes*, his reply text had offered—I hadn't expected to feel so nervous about this meeting, but my heart rate said that I was more anxious than I'd cared to admit. But why?

My expectations were realistic enough; I didn't think he'd instantaneously experience a glorious revelation as a result of my powerful, magical words. And even though I really hoped that Alley would tell me about what he was doing with the company and why, he had no reason to share any of that with me. So, to summarize, I didn't expect him to take my words to heart, and I didn't think he'd tell me anything, either. So what was the point of this thing in the first place? (Breathe . . . two . . . three . . . four.)

Because I told Jimmy I would. And, besides, it was worth a shot.

As it turned out, Alley was more than eager to tell his story.

I sat down in the chair facing Alley's desk. Our requisite smalltalk greetings were pleasant enough, and then I offered the opening salvo into a more substantive give-and-take.

"I like that new paint job in the lobby," I said, flexing my passive-aggressive muscles a little too obviously.

"Okay, look," he said, clearly getting my reference to the fact that he'd covered over the *Do What You Love* quote, which had stood for years as a declaration to all visitors that this company stood for something special.

"I have every right to establish my own priorities as the CEO of this company. And once I took the reins, I needed to clear the slate and set a new direction around here. I had to do what I told the board I would do and do what I believed would get us the best results and put us in the strongest possible position to sell the company and bring a windfall to the shareholders—which, by the way, includes a lot of the employees. That is my number-one motivation, Steve. Not that I need to tell you any of this."

"No, you don't," I said. "But I appreciate your willingness to do so. That means a lot."

"Yeah, well, whatever. You recommended me to this company, so I figure I owe you an explanation."

"Well, you don't. But I appreciate it anyway," I said, meaning it. "But let me ask you something, Alley,"

I continued with a small, conspiratorial smile. "Are you saying your ego has nothing to do with this? That you're not pounding your chest just a bit and . . . I don't know . . . marking your territory?"

It's amazing how I can get away with being so direct when I say things with a wink and a smile.

"My ego?" He paused. "Of course it has to do with my ego. I'm Valley Alley—and I'm proud of that moniker. I earned it.

"Listen, I've got a great track record with what I've accomplished so far, and everyone knows it. But for the first time, I'm in the driver's seat. XinoniX is my chance to prove what I can do as a CEO. That's what I want to be known for, and I will succeed no matter what."

"Okay, I get that," I said. I considered my next words carefully and decided to go with the direct approach.

"But you betrayed Janice's trust in order to get that position, didn't you?"

"I absolutely did not," he said, his face reddening.

I'd clearly hit a nerve.

"She was slacking off," he said. "*She* was betraying the *team's* trust by not leading the way she should have, and I stepped up to fill in the void."

"So you're the white knight then, riding in on your valiant steed to save the day," I said, again with a smile.

"Goddamn right," he said, stiffly. "And proud to do it—for myself, sure, but mostly for the team members who've invested so much time and energy into this place."

"For the team," I repeated, likely sounding as skeptical as I felt.

"Yes. For the team."

We sat and looked at each other for a couple of beats while a tense silence filled the space between us.

"I hear you, Alley. I really do," I said. "Obviously, Janice's leadership needed some mending. And you clearly have very strong opinions about how a company should be run. And, setting aside for a moment the discussion about how you got that job, as the CEO, you have every right to run the show as you see fit."

"That's what I'm saying, Steve. I have an obligation to . . ."

"Hold on," I interrupted, putting up my hand. "I'm not finished."

He looked surprised by my sudden forthrightness.

"You're forgetting one crucial thing, Alley."

"What's that?" He didn't quite roll his eyes, but he might as well have.

"The team that you're ostensibly doing all this for? They're the ones who wove their values into the culture. They're the ones who integrated LEAP into their performance appraisals. They're the ones who love praising each other for modeling those values, and they're the ones who've been compensated with that stock you mentioned by how well they've applied those values to the way they work with each other and with clients.

"These are their values. They own them; they believe in them. It's who they are. And then you came along and summarily and dramatically disregarded and discarded those values—literally, in some cases. And they're frustrated and disheartened and their work is suffering as a result. Why? Because you've told them that they don't matter."

"I'm not telling them they have to forget all that," said Alley. "I'm just . . ."

"Yes, you are," I cut him off. "That's exactly what you're telling them. You're saying that your priorities, your values, are in—and theirs are out. And you're telling them that through your actions, aren't you?

"You've painted over quotes on the wall, removed any reference to LEAP on the company website, and rewritten performance evaluations, to name a few things."

"Okay, yes," said Alley with a hint of a smile. "But, again—that's my right as the leader of this company."

"Sorry," I said. "That's not effective leadership. You're just imposing your will, which is an easy thing to do when you have authority. You've taken the microphone—metaphorically speaking—and launched into a monologue. *The new XinoniX world, according to Alastair Langstrom*. But leadership is a dialogue, not a monologue—it's a give-and-take, a conversation, a sharing of ideas and perspectives in order to arrive at something inclusive, something that people feel like they're a part of. If you leave dialogue out of the equation, you're left with the cynical version of two-way communication: I talk; you listen. And you're right back to people feeling discounted and becoming disengaged."

"Consensus is no way to run a business," Alley said through clenched teeth, the color in his face rising again. "I don't have time—we don't have time—to sit around and talk to each other all day long. And we're certainly not taking a vote on every damn thing."

"Of course not. That's not what I'm saying. You still have to make the big decisions and set the direction and strategic priorities and all that. But don't disregard and discard their experience, their history, their success, in the process. You don't have to force them to abandon all of that in order to set a new emphasis and establish fresh priorities. You can honor them and yourself at the same time."

I felt myself getting worked up, so I paused and reminded myself to breathe . . . two . . . three . . . four.

"Agree to disagree," he said dismissively. "They'll get over it."

Wow, I thought. *That went nowhere fast.*

Ever so slightly, Alley swiveled his chair toward the screen on his left—a subtle but clear indication that he was just about done with this festive little get-together.

He pushed his chair back and stood. I took the hint and did the same.

"Let me ask you something, Alley," I said as I picked up my briefcase. "That time we first met in Palo Alto?"

"Yeah? What about it?"

"You told me you would get behind the company's LEAP philosophy."

"No, I didn't. I said I *could*. Which meant I either could or could not."

"Semantics," I said, holding eye contact with him as we stood facing each other. "That clearly was not your implication."

"Listen, Steve. I had no problem with that love culture idea, per se. But I did not commit to it. What was clear, though, was that I needed to imply it in order to get the job."

I was shocked by that bold admission.

"And you're totally fine with that?" I asked, incredulous.

"Of course. Totally. Everyone plays that game when they're being interviewed. And if you don't believe that, Mr. Leadership Consultant, you're even more naive than I thought you were."

Yowch.

"And to be perfectly clear, you also asked me about my leadership philosophy, did you not?"

I had.

"And do you remember what my answer was?"

I did.

"Remind me," I said anyway.

"It's not personal; it's business," said Alley.

I shook my head as I turned to leave.

"Thanks for stopping by," he said as I stepped into the hall.

And he shut the door behind me.

CHAPTER 17

Never underestimate the therapeutic power of a good, swift kick in the pants. Which is what I felt I'd just received as I walked down the hall to the elevator.

"What can I learn from this encounter?" I asked myself, half-aloud, as I punched the down button a little harder than necessary. I knew there was a lesson in this—there always is—but I was going to have to think on this for a while before I could figure that one out. *Alley is a schmuck* was all I was coming up with at the moment.

I left the building and headed out across the parking lot.

"Pssst! Steve! Over here!"

Jimmy Sun was standing in the shadow on the other side of a big black SUV kind of thing, hissing to me in a stage whisper and motioning frantically for me to join him. I walked over and joined him in the shade.

"A little dramatic, isn't it, Jimmy?" I laughed as I stepped up beside him.

He wasn't finding the humor in this film noir scene of his.

"How'd it go with Alley?" he asked, still half-whispering.

I filled him in and did my best to convey the details of our conversation with the utmost in unbiased, nonjudgmental objectivity.

"He's a schmuck," I concluded, in a most unbiased and nonjudgmental way.

"Yeah," said Jimmy shaking his head. "Listen. I'm going to tell you something that I really shouldn't."

"Then don't, Jimmy. Not if it's going to get you in trouble. You've been walking on thin ice as it is."

"I don't care," he said. "I'm leaving. I'm out of here."

"Sorry, not sorry," I smiled. "That's big news, for sure. Where are you going?"

"I got a great offer to go into finance at YSC."

"Wow," I said. "Congrats! Great place. Cat Cassidy's company. I know them well."

"I know you do," said Jimmy. "I may have dropped your name once or twice as I was interviewing."

"Well, I'm glad I could help," I laughed. "Thanks for letting me know."

"You're welcome. It's a great opportunity, but I feel bad about leaving my friends here on this sinking ship." He gestured to the building behind us.

"Well, look, Jimmy," I said. "I know that Alley's no picnic, but the company looks to be doing quite well—it's not exactly the *Titanic*."

"We were doing well. At first. Alley's tenure started out with a bang, for sure. But now . . ."

"Now? Now what?" This was starting to sound ominous.

"I'm not going to show you the latest numbers," he held up his laptop, which he'd been clutching in his left hand. "But I will tell you that XinoniX is in for a very rough ride. And I happen to know that a big layoff is coming soon."

Alley hadn't even hinted at any of this, of course. He's got a great poker face; I'll give him that.

"It breaks my heart to say it," continued Jimmy. "But everything that Janice did—and Jeffers and Garrison before her—is in danger of going 'poof!' and there's certainly nothing I can do about it."

That begged a big question on my part.

"So, Jimmy," I began. "You implored me to have that conversation with Alley. Why? What were you hoping would happen?"

"I don't know. I guess you were a Hail Mary pass."

"So you were hoping that as a result of the persuasive magnitude of my magnificent words, Alley would see the light and correct the error of his ways?"

I sounded more sarcastic than I'd intended and changed my tone as soon as I'd noticed it.

"In all fairness, Jimmy, you can't put all of this bad news—whatever the details are—on Alley's shoulders."

"Oh, yes, I can. And I do. And it's only fair."

"Why's that?"

"Because in his first few months as CEO? When we were smashing it?"

"Yeah?"

"He took all the credit. He said it was because he'd brought discipline to the company and had gotten everyone focused on the right things."

"So he lived by the sword, and he should die by the sword?"

"You want to take all the credit? Fine," said Jimmy, like I'd suddenly become Alley's proxy. "Then you can have all the blame, too."

"The buck stops here," I said, trotting out another choice cliché.

"Yes. Exactly. We had a culture that was rooted in love and appreciation for each other's contributions. He ripped that out. What did he expect would happen?"

He was getting more worked up as he spoke, and, frankly, righteous indignation looked good on the young Jimmy Sun.

"So what did happen? Why the bad numbers?" I asked.

"Well, it's pretty obvious when you look at," said Jimmy, wagging his laptop at me. "First, the creativity of our design and the quality of our work is declining. People just don't care as much. And, consequentially, that great XinoniX zeal and enthusiasm our customers loved so much? Gone. Just gone. So we're losing clients, losing accounts, losing contracts."

Jimmy paused, lost in thought for a moment.

"As for why I asked you to talk to him, Steve? I guess I really just wanted you to hear his attitude firsthand. I wanted you to see that I wasn't making this stuff up or exaggerating my account of what's been happening around here."

"Then mission accomplished," I said. "Now what? Other than you're leaving?"

"Before I give my notice," he said, tapping his right hand on the laptop, "I'm going to show some financial transparency to my key associates."

"Okay," I said, hesitantly.

"And then I'm going to have one last convo with Alley and tell him what I think of his so-called leadership."

"Well, Jimmy," I said.

"Yes?"

"That ought to be some exit interview."

CHAPTER 18

"The Bolt" was a Rollerblading fixture on the three miles of ocean boardwalk between South Mission Beach and North Pacific Beach. On any given morning, you could find him tooling up and back along the San Diego waterfront, decked out in his trademark mirrored sunglasses, multicolored spandex shirt, and baggy Indian pants cinched tight at the ankles. And to top it all off—literally—he wore a headband with three golden Styrofoam lightning bolts on springs that bobbed and boinged in different directions as he moved his head. He was around five-foot-something and flashed his bright, perpetual smile at everyone along his route. He rarely stopped, and when he did it was only to pet someone's pooch. I don't think I ever saw him chatting with another human being, but I often heard him calling out a hearty hello to their canine companions, which gave the distinct impression that he liked dogs more than people.

The Bolt was a local legend, an enigmatic presence who embodied the offbeat character of the neighborhood, with his bouncing lightning and colorful garb. Even though he was a visual delight to the tourists and a familiar sight to the locals, no one seemed to know anything about him.

No one, that is, except me. And Janice.

A couple of days after my Alley encounter, I was sitting outside on the small porch of the ground-floor apartment in Janice's building where she, Jeffers, and I had had our rooftop session. The tenant, Simon Gallman, was not only a friend of Janice but of mine as well. I was hoping he'd show up before I had to head up north for an important meeting.

Simon was my go-to guy whenever I was feeling down or stressed or worried, and right now, in Janice's absence and the aftermath of my encounter with Alley, I was experiencing all the above. If there was anyone who could jolt me out of a funk, it was him.

I heard him before I saw him coming down the street from the direction of the beachfront.

Simon "The Bolt" Gallman ground his wheels to a dramatic stop in front of me as I stood up to greet him with a smile and a chuckle. It was impossible for me—or, I would argue, anyone—to react to him any other way. He just brought out the happy in people.

Simon's mother grew up in India and came to the United States to study, where she met the Swiss-German man who would eventually become Simon's father. The small family moved to New Delhi while Simon was growing up, and by the time the teenage boy and his family moved back to San Diego, the young man had developed a multicultural accent that was a mild and unique blend of German, Indian, and Southern Californian. More important, though, was his resulting world-wise, multicultural perspective that gave him a sharply perceptive view of, and fascination with, people and our varied human conditions.

Even in his skates, Simon stood about six inches lower than me. His muscled chest, biceps, and abs were accented by the colorful spandex shirt that clung tightly to his body like a second skin. You couldn't pay me enough to wear something like that in public. Or in private, for that matter.

He slapped me a high five and then bent over to loosen the laces on his skates and kick them off his feet.

"Another day at the office, done and dusted!" he lilted in his signature accent. "It's good to see you, Farber. C'mon in."

I followed him through the sliding glass door and into the small living area of his one-bedroom apartment on the ground floor of Janice's building. His place was immaculate. The furniture was sparse but classy. A few plush chairs, a small couch, a round stone table, and lots of green and flowering plants accented the room in just the right places.

His walls were adorned with photo after photo of close-up portraits of people's faces—some famous, most not—that he had snapped throughout the years and around the world. It was like a gallery, each picture a work of art. It was, in fact, literally an art display, given that Simon Gallman was a world-renowned photographer known for his expressive black-and-white images of people from all walks of life.

That's right. The Bolt. Simon Gallman. One man, two identities. Move over, Marvel Comics. I'd always thought that was hilarious. I once asked him why he played this silly secret identity game. "It's no secret to me," he'd said. "I know who I am, no matter what clothes I'm wearing."

"Deep," I'd said, letting him off the hook for an actual answer.

My attention was drawn to the photo hanging prominently over an upholstered chair in a corner of the small living room. The subject's scruffy salt-and-pepper goatee was offset by the unmistakable sparkle of his smiling eyes. His shoulder-length hair jutted out from under a beanie with the iconic Santa Cruz skateboard logo sewn on the front. This sun-weathered, friendly face belonged to someone who had been very special to me, indeed.

"I miss him," I said wistfully as Simon puttered around behind me in his kitchen.

"You miss who?" he called from the other room.

To get his answer, Simon walked over and stood beside me.

"Oh . . . Edg," he said, affectionally tapping the frame of the picture. "I miss him, too."

We looked at the picture together and let the thoughtful silence linger for a few moments.

"Well, hell!" Simon exclaimed, breaking our reverie. "It's not like he's dead or anything."

"Yeah, but he's sure acting like it," I huffed.

"Classic Edg," said Simon. "Disappearing for years at a time with nary a peep to his pals."

Edg, of course, was the guy who had introduced me to the LEAP framework a couple of decades before in the very same beach neighborhood in which we now stood. Which meant that Janice—who now owned this building, in this very same beach neighborhood in which we now stood—was part of the legacy that emanated from the dude in this photo.

What an influence he's had, I thought. And not for the first time, I wondered what Edg would have to say about Janice's current predicament, but I had to admit that for now I was thinking more about my own.

"This situation with Janice has kind of thrown me off-kilter," I muttered half to myself as I followed Simon outside to his patio. "I don't know why, but I take this stuff so . . . so *personally*," I said. "My work with Janice is really seeping over into my life."

Simon suddenly spun around to face me, and that's when I realized he was armed to the hilt. Not with a Glock, but with a Nikon. He pointed the lens at my face and, before I could protest, or react, or—more importantly—pose, he fired off a rapid-fire progression of pics of my unsuspecting mug.

"I didn't know I was gonna be modeling today," I laughed. "And me with no hair and makeup technician." Getting snapped by Simon was a big deal, you know. And he'd never taken a picture of me before, so I was taken aback by this impromptu session.

"Take a look at these," said Simon.

He held up the camera so I could see its display screen as he scrolled through the close-ups of my face.

"What do you see?"

"What do you mean?" I said, suspicious of where he was going with this. "I see me. Or are you looking for something more . . . um . . . symbolic?"

"You see you," he repeated, smiling. "Farber the business guy, or Farber in life?"

"Is there a difference?" I asked, trying to dodge what seemed like a setup.

"You tell me—it's your face," Simon said.

"Just me," I said.

"Right," he said. "And you know what?"

"What?"

"I asked you a flawed question: *Farber in business or Farber in life*? You've heard that expression *in business and in life*, right?"

"Of course," I said. "Who hasn't?"

"Exactly. Who hasn't? We've all used that language forever, and we don't give it a second thought. But it's a flawed premise."

"Flawed how?" I asked.

"It implies they're two different things: business and life. In other words, we're saying that business is not life. And if that's the case, what is it? Death?"

I laughed. "Well, I hope not. But I suppose it can feel that way sometimes."

"Maybe metaphorically," he continued. "But life is life—and some of that life we spend at work, in business, and part of that life we spend in our personal sphere of relationships and activities. We play different roles, and have different tasks and priorities in those roles, but we're the same people regardless. Farber is Farber, whatever you're doing."

"And the Bolt is Simon," I chuckled.

"Simon is Simon," he said. "Sometimes as the Bolt, and sometimes as the photog. Point is," he continued, "we've conditioned ourselves to believe that there's a hard wall between work and everything else, and the logical extension of that for some people—maybe for many—is that there's an entirely different set of rules for each scenario. For example, as you've said many times yourself, we want love in every aspect of our personal life. We want to love our kids, our friends, our partners, and we want them to love us. And then we go to work and it no longer applies? It's absurd. We are the same person at home and at work. One life, different roles. And each role we play influences and affects the other. You have an argument with your boss, and then you go home and snap at your kids; your grandfather passes away, and you can't shake off your sadness just because you have an important presentation at work."

"Some people can," I countered. "Or at least seem to."

"Right. They seem to," he said. "Don't get me wrong. Compartmentalizing is necessary sometimes. And some people are really good at it, and it serves them well in the moment to push feelings aside to be able to perform the task at hand. But that's my point. It's the same person managing different roles and none of those roles exists in a vacuum.

"So when you say that the situation with Janice is 'seeping over into your life,' as you put it, you reveal that you're buying into the myth that you're two different people personally and professionally. And you're creating an added level of angst because the *personal* you believes that it shouldn't be feeling anything about what's happening with the *professional* you. But the truth is, you're just *you*.

"So, thinking we have to adhere to one set of values at work and another set at home creates an unnecessary schism in our psyches and engenders confusion when we're trying to figure out how we want to show up in the world or determine what kind of example we're supposed to set for others."

"I have a schism in my psyche?" I said, savoring the alliteration. "That'd make a great T-shirt."

"Or a catchy heading for your social profiles," Simon added on with a laugh.

"The truth is," he continued, "many people find themselves in situations at work where they feel that schism. They perform; they contribute to the team, to the company, to the leader—whatever. But something just doesn't feel right. They're doing what's asked of them. And by all observable measures, they're great associates, and they get stellar evaluations. Yet they often find themselves driving home in the evening and asking themselves how many times they had to compromise their own values to survive the day, and they wonder why they're so unhappy. And they can't wait to get home so they can get back to their 'lives.'"

"*In work and in life*," I said.

"Right. But as we've determined: Life is life. And wallowing in the illusion of a division doesn't solve the problem."

"So what does?"

"There's no one simple answer to that, of course. But I do have a pretty good clue as to what would help."

I raised my eyebrows, encouraging him to continue.

"Years ago, I was doing a photo shoot for a big C-suite executive who needed new headshots for his company's annual report. I was taking pics of him around his office, and it was going okay, but he was kind of stiff and coming off too formal and inaccessible. A stereotypical silverback alpha male kind of vibe. In between poses at his desk, he picked up a sheet of paper and gazed at it silently to himself. I noticed that his eyes sparkled a little, and he smiled, obviously inspired by what he was reading. So I started snapping away to capture the moment."

"That's what makes you a great photographer," I said, thinking about how he'd just done that to me a few minutes before.

"That's true for any decent photog," he said, modestly deflecting the compliment.

"I get great pictures when I can get my subject to talk about something that excites them," Simon continued. "So I asked him to tell me about that paper.

"He turned it around and held it up so I could see what he'd been looking at. It was a crayon drawing of a stick figure daddy and daughter standing under a green and brown tree with a yellow sun radiating from the top right corner of the page. A cute picture, sure. But I'll never forget the conversation that it sparked."

CHAPTER 19

"My daughter drew that for me," the executive said to Simon.

"How old is she?" Simon asked.

"Now? She's twenty-three. She drew this when she was five."

"And you still keep it on your desk? That's lovely," said Simon.

"It's a constant reminder of what's really important. I've come a long way in my career since then," he said. "And I've made some big sacrifices along the way. But I've never wavered from this one priority in my life. Not that I've been the perfect father. But I am always and foremost her dad."

"Even when you're sitting there behind the resolute desk?" asked Simon with a smile.

"Even here," he said. "And I've found that this picture is especially important here at work, not only because it serves as a reminder to me, but because it's a great conversation starter with others."

"How so?" asked Simon, snapping away on his Nikon.

"Well . . . it's happening right now, isn't it? Between us? Same thing happens every day. Someone sits in the chair next to my desk, sees the picture, and asks me about it. That gives me the opportunity to tell my story as a dad—not just the person they see as the big boss. And it gives me the opening to ask them about the priorities in their lives. It's inspiring to see how much people are willing to share if I just give them the opportunity. And we get to know each other as people, not functions. I learn about their values, and they learn about mine. And that's good for everyone."

"Good for everyone? How?" Simon asked as he stepped around the desk to get a different angle.

"You really want to know?" he said. "I'm warning you that I'm kind of a geek on this subject."

"Geek away!" encouraged Simon.

He opened a file drawer in his desk, pulled out an old academic publication from 1993 called *The Journal of Business Ethics*, and leafed through it until he found what he was looking for.

"This study is called 'Values congruence and differences between the interplay of personal and organizational value systems,'" he said, spreading the document out so Simon could see it. "I told you, right? Geek!" he laughed.

"For me, it all started with this particular paper," he continued. "But the bottom line is that several studies, going back a few decades now, show the importance of company values. It's become conventional wisdom. That's why virtually every company has a set of values published on its website and repeated in its annual report. As do we," he pointed to their company values statement hanging on the wall behind him.

"Year after year, study after study has shown that values have an impact on all the things we want our folks to experience when they come to work: job satisfaction, organizational commitment, lower turnover, trust, innovation, readiness to change, performance, motivation—you name it. But most companies overlook the key element in all of this values stuff."

He paused to make sure that Simon wouldn't miss the punchline.

"The cornerstone to all of this is a person's clarity—not about company's values, but about their own."

"Not what's important to the company?"

"Well, yes, that, too. *Congruence* is the degree to which your own personal values align with the company's. The higher the congruence, the better. But here's what they found: Even though the highest level of commitment shows in people who are clear on the organization's values and clear on their own, the second highest commitment level comes from people who are *not* clear on the company's values—they couldn't recite the values statement, for example—but they could tell you what's important to them personally. And they show higher levels of commitment than those who can tell you what the company values are but draw a blank on their own principles.

"So, in my opinion, before trotting out our corporate values, there's a question we should ask first. And we should ask it of everyone."

"Which is?" asked Simon

He held up his daughter's artwork.

"What's important to you in the way you lead your life?" he said. "And when people answer that question—or even try to answer it—it brings everything into sharper focus and shines a brighter light on their own values, hopes, dreams, and aspirations. And then, through that renewed clarity of purpose in their eyes, they look at our corporate values and, maybe for the first time, they see themselves in those words."

"And there's a better chance of greater congruence between their values and the company's?" Simon summarized.

"Which naturally leads to higher commitment," said the executive, picking up the journal and giving it a little wave in the air.

"By the way," said Simon, clicking a few final pics of his subject, who looked much lighter and friendlier than he did at the session's outset. "Whose research was that?"

"Two guys," said the executive geek. "Warren H. Schmidt and . . . wait one second." He leafed through the publication to find the right page. "Ah . . . here it is.

"Barry Z. Posner," he said.

"Well, surprise, surprise," I said to Simon as he wrapped up his story. "The ubiquitous Barry," I chuckled and explained my connection with Herr Professor.

"Well, *that's* pretty cool," said Simon. "I had no idea. Gotta love that synchronicity, right?"

"For sure," I said, shaking my head in wonder. "And, as a matter of fact, getting clear on her personal values is exactly what Jeffers and I asked Janice to do."

I recounted Jeffers's and my rooftop encounter with Janice months before.

"We asked her to get clear on what's important to her and to let people know what those priorities and beliefs are. And I'm hoping that she's doing that right now, wherever she is."

Simon put down his camera and locked his eyes on mine.

"So?" he said. "And?"

"So and what?" I said, confused by the question.

"That's what you asked Janice to do? So? And?" he repeated.

"So, I hope that's what she's doing," I repeated, still befuddled.

"So," he sighed with a dramatic eyeroll, "are *you* doing what you said *she* should do?"

"Am I rediscovering my own values and beliefs?"

"Yes. Are you? Seems to me that you and Janice have a similar path to walk. You both would serve yourselves well by rediscovering what matters most to you personally."

"I don't think I need to. I'm a fairly self-aware dude."

"And yet you have a schism in your psyche," said Simon with a smile.

CHAPTER 20

Over the next few weeks, my discussion with Simon sent me careening down the proverbial memory lane as I revisited my two-decades-long journey into the Extreme Leadership approach to business and beyond. Note that I didn't say to "business and life." Yeah, I've always been a good student.

I'd thought back to the first day I'd met the surfer dude Edg, as I was sitting on the seawall of the Mission Beach boardwalk. He'd introduced me to the Radical LEAP framework and then taken me under his wing (do surfers have wings?) to give me a lightning-fast education that expanded my perspective on leadership and quite literally shifted the trajectory of my life. Now, after twenty-five years of a second marriage, several books, original music recordings, a fulfilling career, and a passel of kids and step-kids released as full-fledged, self-actualized adults into the wilds of the world (and a few grand-kids, too), I asked myself this question: Are Love, Energy, Audacity, and Proof still at the core of who I am, what I believe in, and how I make a difference in the world around me?

The answer, as you may have guessed, was unequivocally yes. If anything, my understanding of and belief in those tenets had only deepened and strengthened through experience and loads (and I mean *loads*) of trial and error both in my business and in my lif . . . I mean, in all spheres of my life, including my work, family, friendships, and volunteer efforts. Life is life, and, for me, then and now, LEAP was my meaningful way to navigate through all of it.

Perhaps that sounds obvious, but even though my conclusion didn't surprise me, my renewed sense of energy did. And along with that energy surge came my revitalized commitment to being the best model I could humanly be of the very things I've been asking others to do.

I thought about The Radical Promise that Jim, Barry, and I had penned. I thought about Janice's despondency and the assignment Jeffers had given her to write her Credo Memo, and I was once again struck by the tremendous value and power of aligning words and actions. In order to Do What You Say You Will Do, you first have to get very, very clear on what it is that you *say* is important.

After all, isn't that why people renew their wedding vows?

I've always found it inspiring when couples take the time to renew their vows to each other. It's their way of saying, *After all we've been through together, you and I, we take this moment to remind each other of our mutual love, devotion, and commitment, and we reaffirm that we still mean it.*

The *Oxford English Dictionary* defines "vow" as "a solemn promise, or a set of promises committing one to a prescribed role, calling or course of action." That's a nice thing to reaffirm with your life partner, right?

But here's the thing: I never hear of people renewing vows to themselves. For most of us, there's nothing to renew because we never vowed anything to begin with. I know I never had. Not really. So, given my rebirthed jolt of committed exuberance, I thought that it would be a good time to make a vow to myself.

I took a field trip back to Mission Beach, back to the boardwalk, and back to that seawall where I had perched on that fateful day when Edg swooped into my life.

For a few minutes I watched the waves slap up against the shore, and then I took out my Wake-Up Pad and wrote these words to myself:

> "As of now, I recommit to a calling rooted in Love to transform the particulars of my life. From this day forward I will, with every bit of Energy and Audacity that I can muster, approach my relationships, my work, and my activities with the expressed intent of changing everything I touch for the better. The Proof of my success will be the legacy that I leave, the imprint that I make, and the people I boost up along the way. From time to time, if I fall short of the mark or even fail completely, I won't have the slightest residue of regret because my intent will always be noble. I will LEAP, and it will be exhilarating."

I dismounted from the seawall, kicked off my flip-flops, and walked ankle-high in the water along the ocean's edge for a mile up to Pacific Beach and then returned along the bay. It was a loop I had walked countless times back in the days I had lived in the bayside building that now belonged to Janice.

I noticed a little more bounce in my step than I'd felt lately, but I also had a heightened sense of concern for Janice. Radio silence was not her kind of thing. At least it hadn't been. It had been nearly half a year since she went away, and I'd only gotten an occasional text letting me know that she was still, indeed, alive. She was doing well, she'd said, and that I shouldn't worry. I did feel relieved at first, but that text was a few months ago, now. And from what I could gather, none of her remaining former colleagues at XinoniX had heard from her, either. I felt my concern resurging.

And given the vow I'd just made to myself—boosting others up, and all that—her absence frustrated me because I felt even more committed to aiding Janice in her triumphant, phoenix-like emergence from the ashy depths of despair.

But it was already too late for me to help.

CHAPTER 21

Later that evening, after I'd returned home from the muse-like influence of the Mission Beach neighborhood, I was shocked to receive a text from Janice. It was as though she had been eavesdropping on my brain during my internal vow-renewal conversation and took that opportunity to finally reach out to me.

"Please meet me tomorrow," said the glowing text on my iPhone. It then gave me a time and a local San Diego address. And that was it. No context and no more information—other than a tiny folded-hand emoji. Its sparseness reminded me of that text I'd received from Jeffers when he'd heard about Alley coming to XinoniX. And not in a good way.

Yes, I was relieved to have received proof of life. But given that I hadn't heard from Janice in ages, and that I hadn't even known she was back in town, I must admit I was feeling more irritated than anything else.

I activated the sarcasm nerves in my thumbs and replied.

"Well, well, as I live and breathe. If it isn't my long-lost friend," I texted. "As luck would have it, I'm available then. You wanna tell me anything else?" I touched *send* and waited for an explanation.

"Yes," she replied.

I waited expectantly for her next text while the little ellipses danced on my screen.

"Suite 108," it said.

I laughed, seeing that she was clearly messing with me by playing up the silly mystery of this whole exchange.

Typical, I thought, allowing myself to feel more amused than annoyed. *Okay, I'll bite.*

I hopped over to my friend Mr. Google, typed in the address and suite number, and saw that the office belonged to a company called Pacific Horizons. According to their company website, they specialized in integrated logistics solutions, moving freight between the mainland and key ports across the Pacific. Their fleet of trucks, containers, and chartered vessels created a seamless bridge between businesses and their destinations. They handled everything from door-to-door transportation to customs clearance and warehousing, with a particular expertise in complex supply chain management for mid-sized companies expanding into Asian markets.

I knew next to nothing about that industry, and I had no idea why Janice had asked to meet me there. Maybe she needed to ship something? Was she planning on moving overseas?

Curious, I dug a little deeper into Pacific Horizons and learned that the company's history read like a cautionary business tale—near financial collapse and a revolving door of leadership resulting in organizational whiplash that left employees disillusioned and the company teetering on the edge of permanent closure. Their Glassdoor profile was crammed with a fetid pile of negative employee reviews, and their customer ratings on Yelp and elsewhere weren't any better.

If Janice was looking for a company to ship her valued belongings somewhere, I couldn't for the life of me imagine why she'd chosen this place.

But, of course, I had it all wrong.

CHAPTER 22

The unassuming office structure was just down the street from the San Diego airport. As I pulled into the parking lot, I saw a food truck offering Mexican fare parked alongside the sidewalk near the building's entrance. It was nearly lunchtime, and the idea of a fresh California burrito rang a loud bell in my stomach as I walked past and caught a whiff of the grill.

Inside the building, I squinted to adjust to the lower light, got my bearings, and quickly found the entry to suite 108. I expected to see a sign for Pacific Horizons, so I was more than a little confused when, instead, I saw the name "WG Maritime Shipping Masters" printed on a sheet of paper taped to the door above the number.

I had briefly met WG "Pops" Maritime a couple of decades earlier when my friend Edg had introduced me to the business legend. Maritime had built a business empire with enterprises in a wide variety of markets, from boat leasing to food service to industrial steam cleaning, before suddenly cashing it all in and retiring to live out his final days in peace. My short and immensely consequential conversation with him had set me resolutely on my path to pursuing Love as a hard-core business principle.

"Relationships in the world of business are won," Pops had said to me, "by proving through your own actions that you really love your customers, your colleagues, and your employees."

And the words "Do what you love in the service of people who love what you do," which had adorned the walls in the XinoniX corporate office—until Alley had obliterated them with a fresh coat of paint—were, in fact, his.

The befuddled look on my face must have been quite the sight to behold. As I tentatively reached for the knob, the door suddenly swung open and there stood a beaming Janice with arms outstretched in greeting.

I can only imagine what that additional surprise did to the already cartoonish expression on my mug.

"Welcome!" she exclaimed with a laugh, clearly delighting in my shock. "C'mon in, Farber!"

She took me by the hand and led me down the hallway into an open bullpen area where a couple of dozen folks with headsets were sitting or standing at their desks and chattering away into their mics as they tapped on their computer keyboards. I assumed they must have been talking with customers, but whatever they were doing, they seemed to be having a great time; the fun, upbeat energy in the air was palpable. I stood blinking in amazement as Janice waved her arms around to catch everyone's attention.

Little by little, the conversations ended, the people quieted down, and they turned their focus to Janice.

"Hey, team!" said Janice. "This is my good friend, Steve Farber. So whaddaya say we give him a big WG Maritime special welcome?"

The group erupted with whoops and laughter, and before I could sort out what was happening, they started pelting me with Nerf balls, which, apparently, they had stashed in buckets under their desks.

"Well, it's nice to meet you, too," I shouted as I picked up a few of the foam armaments and returned a volley as best I could. The pandemonium faded as quickly as it had started, and the group erupted into a standing ovation in my honor.

And before you could say *haze the visitor,* they went back to their calls. Other than some lingering chuckles and a few shouts of *welcome* in my direction, it was as if nothing out of the ordinary had ever happened. The playfulness, joy, and outright goofiness of that offbeat encounter both delighted and surprised me.

"What the hell is going on, Janice?" I laughed.

I mean, seriously, this was my kind of silliness, and I found it all hilarious. But still . . . what the *hell*?

"Welcome, my friend," she crooned as she led me around the floor past a row of glass-paned offices, "to Janice Everson's Next Big Adventure."

I shook my head in amazement, which looked to her like confusion, I guess.

"I've started a new company," she said, as though I'd missed the punchline.

"Well, yeah, I can see that," I laughed.

"And we're building a culture here that's both playful and productive—and we're doing it in all kinds of ways. The Nerf ball thing erupted between a few folks one day—I'm not even sure what precipitated it—and it became an instant 'initiation' ritual. Of course, there's a lot more to it, and I promise I'll tell you the whole story. But first, allow me to introduce you to my partner."

At the end of the office hallway, we stepped through an arched doorway and out into a lovely little courtyard filled with potted palms and colorful flowering plants.

She motioned to the person sitting at a lattice-topped table in the middle of the space—a person whom, of course, I recognized immediately.

"Well," I said. "The hits just keep on coming, don't they?"

CHAPTER 23

Cat Cassidy stood to greet me as I walked across the courtyard. My head turned side to side to look repeatedly at each of the women as though I were watching a tennis match at close range.

"Okay, look," I said to them. "I know you two are having all kinds of fun right now at my expense, but . . ." I focused my attention on Janice. "You disappeared, like, a hundred years ago, and other than the occasional cryptic text, you pretty much ghosted me. And you clearly have not been lying on a remote beach this whole time." I swept my arms around to indicate the place in which we were standing.

"And you!" I pointed to Cat. The mischievous glee radiating from her face was annoying the crap out of me. "Can we please dispense with the fun and games for a second and fill me in on just what exactly the flying fructose is going on here?"

I plopped petulantly into a chair and beseeched the two of them to join me.

As they sat, Cat stretched her hand toward Janice.

"Take it away, girl," she said.

"Of course," said Janice. "I'm happy to give you all the glorious details, Steve."

"Thank you," I said, relieved. "Tell me the whole story."

And it's about damn time, I said to myself. I folded my hands in my lap and waited for her to begin.

Janice stared at me in silence.

"What?" I shouted.

"Say *please*," she said.

"Oh, for fu—okay . . . pul-*leeze*," I drew the word out like a toddler begging for a cookie.

"That's better," she laughed.

"Well," she began. "I guess it all became clear to me one morning in the rainforest of Costa Rica."

And, for once, I kept my mouth shut while she spoke.

CHAPTER 24

"As you know, I went away to try to heal from my emotional and psychological stress. I expected it to be hard work; what I didn't expect was that I'd also get a case of shingles. I thought that was a sickness for, you know, old people. I was too young for that. But I was wrong, and it hit me with a vengeance. And, let me tell you, I wouldn't wish that disease on anyone—even Alley. But to deal with the incessant, excruciating pain, I forced myself to walk along the trails through the fragrant air and beautiful music of the jungle. And as I did, it became evident to me that the outbreak was just my body reacting to the strain and stress of losing my company. And that meant I had to let XinoniX go.

"*Just let it go.* I must have said that to myself a thousand times. I tried multiple variations on the theme: *What's done is done, you can't change the past, everything happens for a reason*—all kinds of words like that. But *let it go* soon became my mantra and, little by little, I started to believe that I could.

"And then one day, I noticed that my rashes had subsided, and the pain in my skin had eased up. And for the first time, I felt—what's the word—*liberated*. It wasn't that I was looking at the past through rose-colored glasses, but I was able to review the experience and, maybe for the first time, ask myself what I'd learned from it. I was able to allow myself to appreciate all my successes and review my mistakes without the loads of emotional baggage I'd been carrying around.

"It was like I became my own case study, and I analyzed that story with all the intensity and clarity of a star MBA student. I knew what I had done right; I knew where I had screwed up. I'd let my priorities get muddled, and I'd assumed that the culture of the company and my own personal credibility had been established and set in stone. I thought it no longer required my personal vigilance and attention. So much so that even in the face of all the warning signs and deep conversations with you, Steve—as well as with Jim, and Barry, and Cat—I fatally discounted the value of my daily personal example and influence and let my focus go elsewhere.

"I certainly don't regret the time I spent and the difference I made with the nonprofit, but I just did a terrible job of balancing my commitments there with my responsibilities at the company. And the list goes on. Most important, though, was that I knew what I'd do differently if I were to start all over again.

"And that's when it hit me: That's what I needed to do. *Start all over again*. Obviously, I couldn't do that at XinoniX, even if I'd wanted to. Besides, rebuilding my credibility there after it'd been so damaged would be more daunting a task than I'd care to take on. So, anyway, I wanted to start fresh, with a clean slate. I needed to finally say farewell to XinoniX in my heart and begin again from scratch.

"I'd start a new company, maybe. Or maybe buy a failing one and rebuild it. It didn't matter. As long as I could apply all the lessons I'd learned in my life so far and do it right and create something fun, and meaningful, and wildly successful in every way.

"I was also clear that I couldn't—and didn't want to—do this alone. I needed an experienced partner. Someone who'd been there, business-wise. And someone who shared my values and priorities. Someone who was committed to the power and promise of operationalizing Love in the way business is conducted. Someone who was credible to the core, who lived a life of action that was congruent with their deeply held beliefs. In the abstract, that was the kind of person I needed. But who, specifically, could it be?

"And right then, an image of that specific person leapt into my mind. I knew it was a long shot that she'd be interested in partnering with me in any way. I mean, it wasn't like Cat Cassidy was sending out her résumé and looking for a job. She was the superstar CEO of YSC, for goodness' sake. But at the very least, I knew she'd be a great sounding board, and maybe she could help me think things through as I sought out the right opportunity to pursue and the right people to pursue it with.

"Cat and I had gotten together several times since that night you'd first introduced us at Boudin's Bar, and our friendship had been growing. We were at ease with each other; in sync, philosophically speaking. Mostly, we'd stayed in touch by text, but this time I wanted to hear her voice—and I wanted for her to hear mine, to hear my conviction, my resolve. So, while sitting on my balcony facing into the Costa Rican rainforest, I popped in my earbuds and touched her number on my cell.

"As I filled her in on my nascent idea, I, of course, didn't expect her to commit to working with me. And, of course, she didn't. But she was extremely encouraging and supportive, and she promised to help in any way she could. She offered to get together with me whenever I got back to San Diego, which until that moment, I'd had no plans to do any time soon.

"And as soon as we ended our call, I booked my flight home.

"The next evening, Cat picked me up at the San Diego airport. There was something she'd wanted to show me, she'd said, and it would be easier for us to drive there together. I threw my bags in the flat bed of her Rivian truck and slid into the passenger seat. She handed me an old-school loose-leaf binder with a label saying 'Pacific Horizons' affixed to the cover. I leafed through the company dossier as we zipped off silently past the terminal and down the street around the bay. Five minutes later, we arrived at the building where we're sitting right now."

CHAPTER 25

I had been miffed that Janice hadn't stayed in touch with me. But now, after hearing about her trying emotional and physical journey, I felt more proud of her than anything else. And I was so happy to see the renewed spark in her eyes and hear the energy in her voice.

She had been through the proverbial dark night of the soul and emerged—where? At a shipping company?

"Thank you so much for sharing your story with me, my friend," I said. "It means a lot to me that you did. And I'm so glad you're back. But . . ." I stopped myself mid-sentence and tried to rein myself in. I had so many questions.

"But why this business?" I spewed. "A shipping company? What do you know about this industry? And are you two partners in this venture? And what about YSC, Cat?" I couldn't stop my unabashed query vomit, so I was relieved when Cat jumped in.

"Okay," she laughed. "You have lots of questions. We get it. The quick answer is that I'd been looking at Pacific Horizons for a long time. I had been wanting to diversify my personal business portfolio, and I thought a turnaround opportunity would be a fun challenge as long as I had the right people and the right scenario to work with. I wasn't about to leave YSC—and I don't know if I ever will—but I really liked the idea of taking a failing company and resurrecting it from the ashes. I mean, that sounds like a blast, doesn't it?"

"I could see why you'd think so, knowing you," I smiled.

"So, when Janice called me that day," Cat continued, "it all just kind of clicked for me. It was perfect timing, really. Janice could be the operational partner that I'd need and Pacific Horizons had *opportunity* written all over it."

"Because of your deep combined expertise in shipping and logistics?" I said with my trademark sarcasm.

Cat ignored me, of course, and explained that Pacific Horizons had first come to her attention when one of YSC's executive recruiters had placed a new CEO with the company. And six months later, YSC was again contracted to replace that CEO with another one. Two chief executives in as many months did not bode well for that company, so, curious about their client, Cat had taken a closer look. And, not surprisingly, she found that PH had—to put it nicely—a toxic waste dump of a culture. The shipping company was founded in 2011 to move barges of containers of goods back and forth across the seas to various parts of the United States and beyond. Not a bad business when your clients were the likes of big retail chains and individual private customers, too. But somehow, over the past decade, PH had managed to reach revenues of $100 million with an annual operating loss of $24 million. They had 120 employees and a 30% turnover rate, which required spending piles of money on recruiters to keep the place staffed.

And two CEOs in two months wasn't the whole C-suite story, either. They had in fact burned through a total of four CEOs in four years and four VPs of HR in the same time period. Their customer satisfaction numbers were abysmal, too. Which was why, in order to get said customers, they had to slash their prices year after year. All of that added up to being a low-cost provider on the brink of bankruptcy, which therefore led to their board's frantic search for a heroic CEO who would take the helm mid-storm and—pun intended—right the ship.

"So I bought the company," said Cat in a manner so matter of fact it made me laugh. "Janice had liked what I'd shown her that evening, and I could tell that she was seeing the same challenge and opportunity that I saw. So I negotiated a buyout with the board, brought Janice in as my partner, and for all intents and purposes, handed the reins to her."

"As the CEO of Pacific Horizons?" I asked.

"Well, no," said Janice. "I thought the CEO title had too much of a negative connotation with the employees, so I opted for the title of president instead. I figured I'd earn the CEO designation after I'd proven myself to the team."

"Smart," I said. "So when was that?"

"Well, um . . . about six months ago," said Janice, hesitantly.

"What?" I exclaimed. "Six months you've been here?" I was having a hard time getting my head around the fact that they'd chosen to keep me in the dark all this time.

"I know," said Janice, earnestly. "You'll forgive me, right? I really needed to start this under the radar. I hope you'll understand once you've seen what we've been able to accomplish in such a short period of time."

"I'm all ears," I said.

"Okay!" said Cat as she excused herself to head back to YSC. "You guys have fun . . . let the tour begin!"

CHAPTER 26

We said our goodbyes to Cat and walked around the bullpen for quite a while as Janice introduced me to several members of the team. Almost to a person, they seemed happy and friendly and eager to talk about their experience. Many had been with the company for ten or more years, so they'd seen and experienced the transition from the olden days to life under Janice's leadership. As I chatted with folks from a variety of functions—including customer service, logistics, fleet management, and accounting—I saw a clear pattern emerging. From the minute she'd walked through the doors as the new CEO (I mean president), Janice was on a mission to create tangible signs of both the preexisting and new values she was determined to instill in the culture. Some of the things she did were symbolic, others systemic. And with only a couple of grumpy exceptions—people who obviously wanted things to stay the way they'd always been—everyone seemed clear on the new cultural imperative: to create a place that they loved working in and that customers loved doing business with.

I had the overwhelming sense that this was a great turnaround story in the making. And I was excited for all of them.

"You have a terrific team here," I said to Janice after a couple of hours of deep and, from what I could surmise, truthful conversations with the folks.

We were standing in the common area next to a foosball table and popcorn machine, and several people gathered around us as we spoke.

"Thank you," said Janice. "Now you see why I wasn't concerned about my inexperience in the industry. These people are the experts." She motioned to the group, which was growing by the minute. Soon we had quite a crowd listening in on our conversation. And I've always loved a live studio audience.

"This team is the best there is," Janice continued. "But they'd been held back by a micromanaged, autocratic environment. And everyone—including the customers and shareholders—suffered as a result."

I noticed quite a few nodding heads.

"My only job is to unleash their capacity, to give them what they need to shine. And they were starving for it. But I was the new kid in town. I had zero credibility when I first walked through the door of suite 108. I knew I had to prove myself to them right away. So, first of all, I started carrying this."

She tapped on a notebook, which, I now realized, she'd had with her the whole time.

"My commitment journal. I started cultivating my contractual attitude from the first minute."

"Nice!" I said, feeling a pang of guilt that mine was sitting on my desk at home.

"I also had to earn their trust by showing them who I was and by learning who they were. And what's the quickest way to start getting to know people? You learn their names," Janice said without waiting for me to answer.

Apparently, she explained, it had been a long-standing policy at the company that everyone had to wear a name badge at all times. No one knew why, but a rule's a rule, right?

"We were a small company," Janice said with a shrug. "At the very least, shouldn't we know each other's names? So you know what we did? We abolished the name tags."

"And you know what Janice did?" someone in the group piped in.

"She memorized all of our names—all 120 of us," someone else answered with a laugh.

"Okay . . . you could say that banishing the badges was only a symbolic gesture, but learning everyone's name was more than that." She looked around at the gathered group. "It was my simple way of showing you that I cared, and that I wanted to get to know you all—because I did. Now, let me ask you guys . . . why is that important?"

"Because it meets the Cred Standard," several responded in unison, which brought a good-natured laugh from the others.

"The Credibility Standard," I extrapolated, smiling.

"Right," she said. "It's a filter that we put everything through. For example, when we say we want people to love working here, we just ask, *Is this love?* when analyzing our actions, when determining what we do, or what we should do instead. Are name badges *love*? Nope. Is knowing everyone's name by heart? Yup."

"I love that," I said, aware of my word choice. "Can you give me some more examples?"

"I don't know . . . can we?" Janice laughed as she panned her gaze across the team.

"Well, just look around, for starters," said a tall guy dressed in jeans and a pressed T-shirt. "See this foosball table? New. Popcorn machine? New. Ice machine? Kombucha keg? All new. In fact, we designed this whole common area for one reason: to bring us all together, to allow for us to talk to each other. That's how we become friends, not just co-workers. And if we all have friends that we enjoy hanging out with, we're more likely to love coming to work every day."

"Well said," Janice encouraged. "Now, this may not seem like a big deal in a lot of other companies, especially in the Googles and tech start-ups of the world. But in contrast to this company's deeply siloed and compartmentalized past, it's a very big deal here."

"And look across the room," she continued, pointing in the direction of the parking lot. "You can see all the way to the front door, right?"

"Of course," I said.

"That's because we lowered the height of the cubicle dividers to below eye level. They used to be floor to ceiling, so you know what that meant?"

"We never talked to the people sitting right next to us," chirped a voice from the studio audience.

"Tell him about the shipping policy," someone called out.

"Yes, tell me about the shipping policy," I echoed eagerly.

"For years," said Janice, "the policy of this company had been that we would not ship a barge unless it was at least 75% full. Anything less than that and we'd lose money on that shipment. So if all you do is look at the ledger sheet and make your decision on that basis, it would make no sense to sail. After all, we're not in the business to lose money, right?

"But we took another look at that long-standing sacred cow of a policy and reevaluated it from the customer's perspective. Say, for example, you're shipping a car to your niece in Acapulco, and you've told her it would arrive on a specific date, because that's what we told you when you booked the shipment. But that day comes and goes and still no car. So you call us to find out what happened, and we tell you the car is still in the container on the barge at the dock in San Diego because we haven't sold enough space yet. What's your reaction gonna be?"

"I'd be apoplectic," I said with no exaggeration.

"Of course you would. So we put that policy through the Cred Standard filter and asked this question: Given that same scenario, on that same promised shipping date, if we really loved our customer, what would we do? And then the answer was pretty obvious, wasn't it?" she said to the group.

"We would sail," someone called out.

"We would sail," Janice repeated.

"And from that moment on, our new policy was and remains really simple: We sail when we said we would sail. If we didn't sell enough space on that barge, that's our problem, not our customers'."

"DWYSYWD," I said.

"Exactly," said Janice. "That's the essence of the Cred Standard."

"But you still lose money on those shipments. That doesn't change just because you're suddenly being congruent with your values."

"And we did lose money—at first. And I'd be lying if I said I didn't lose a few nights of sleep over it. But we had faith that it wouldn't stay that way. And we were right. It took some time to move the needle, but here we are less than a year later, and we're always at least 95% full on all our shipments."

"Because your reputation changed," I surmised.

"Right. Remember, we had a terrible track record with customers. Our customer reviews were pitiful. But not anymore. We're getting new customers, and it's starting to reflect on the bottom line across the board.

"We take all of our values and put everything we do through the Cred Standard filter: Is this love? Is this reliability? Is this attention to detail? If the answer is no, we either ditch it or change it."

She then went through a quick litany of all the new and improved systems, policies, procedures, and traditions they were now doing as a result of using the Cred Standard filter—including the Nerf ball bombardment I had experienced when I arrived, which was the result of a few people who'd decided they wanted to show visitors (including interviewees) that this place was different—and fun. And a new ritual was born.

That made me think about a couple of the less enthusiastic people I'd talked to earlier.

"And everyone was good with all this change?" I asked, looking across the faces of the folks gathered around us.

"Well, no," said Janice. "We did have some resistors who were set firmly in the old ways. So I had to let more than a few people go. But we were kind. And we were helpful in finding them new opportunities, if they were open to it. And we still have a few who are either adjusting or deciding whether they want to adapt or leave. And either choice is fine. This cultural shift is not without its challenges, of course. And it's not for everyone."

I admired the transparency she was demonstrating by speaking honestly about this in the current public forum.

"But here's the flipside," Janice continued, her face brightening. "Do you want to know how much money we spend on recruiters now?"

"You mean like Cat's company?" I asked.

Janice laughed.

"Right. Like YSC . . . and others."

"How much?"

She formed a "zero" with her fingers and held it up in front of her face.

"These are our best recruiters, right here," she said, gesturing to the group. "And that," Janice said, her voice choking ever so slightly, "is the best testimonial of all."

We wound our conversation down and the crowd dispersed, with many of them heading for the door. It was a late lunchtime, I presumed.

"It's food-truck day," said Janice. "We do it once a week and buy lunch for anyone who wants. A different truck each time. And the only rule is that if you eat from the truck, you have to have your meal with someone from the company you don't know very well."

"You're creating something very special here, my friend," I said, feeling deeply happy for her, and, given what she'd gone through, more than a bit relieved. She walked with me toward the door.

"Oh, one more thing," Janice snapped her fingers, remembering something important. "We're relaunching the company with a grand reopening and an official name change."

"WG Maritime Shipping Masters," I said, recalling the paper taped to the door of the office suite. I had meant to ask about that.

"I hope it'll be a fitting tribute to Pops's legacy," Janice said with a smile.

"Do what you love in the service of people who love what you do," I said over my shoulder as I walked out the door.

And with great anticipation emanating from my stomach, I headed to the food truck for a fresh California burrito with soon-to-be new friends.

CHAPTER 27

While dawn was spreading over the reborn WG Maritime enterprise, across town in Sorrento Valley, dark clouds had descended on XinoniX.

It had been months since Jimmy Sun departed the company and went to work for Cat, just as he had told me he would do that day in the parking lot. But not before starting a tsunami.

The first tremor had been felt when, later that same day, Jimmy had taken his laptop back to his office and emailed the latest company numbers to . . . well, the whole company. He had told me he was going to share it with "key associates." For Jimmy Sun, that meant everybody:

> Dear friends and colleagues,
> In the interest of living up to Alley's dedication to the importance of our bottom-line financials and his commitment to being transparent with those numbers, I'm

sharing with all of you our latest analysis and forecast. I invite you to spend some time with this and to draw your own conclusions, but it seems painfully clear to me that we're going to miss our revenue targets by a wide margin, and the budget implications are severe.

Our customer satisfaction numbers have dropped precipitously, as have our quality scores—and that's having a direct impact on our sales numbers. In my opinion, I believe these statistics are a result of the change in our experience of working at this company we once loved. We're just not caring like we used to, and our attention to detail is not what it once was. People are scared to speak up, and when fear creeps in we withdraw and try to protect our own turf. And then we stop talking to each other. We stop helping each other to learn from our mistakes, and we no longer share knowledge and information.

As you review the attached spreadsheets and consider the implications for you and your career, I suggest that you either figure out how to reignite your personal passion for this post-LEAP company or find another place that you can.

I think you can surmise what I'm going to do by the fact that I'm sending you this email without Alley's knowledge or consent. And I accept any and all consequences for having done so.

Your friend and soon to be former colleague,

Jimmy Sun,

Finance

As you can well imagine, Alley blew his lid when he read that email. And I can't say that I blame him. While I understood Jimmy's motive for sending that missive, I had mixed feelings about it. On the one hand, by being so brutally candid, Jimmy used Alley's espoused value of "transparency" as a kind of weapon against him. Maybe Jimmy could have been more diplomatic in his approach or more sensitive to the impact it would have on his "friends and colleagues" who, after all, still depended on XinoniX for their livelihoods.

On the other hand, I admired his last-ditch attempt to effect some change at XinoniX before he left—or at the very least, to warn the people he cared about, so they could begin to plan accordingly instead of being blindsided when the inevitable layoffs came. Maybe the old Jimmy Sun would have just ridden off quietly into the sunset, but the new Jimmy saw himself as a values warrior who had no choice but to put his beliefs on the public record—even as a parting shot.

And a parting shot it was. Jimmy had thought his last action at XinoniX would be to personally deliver his letter of resignation to Alley and have one last conversation with him before he left. He had planned exactly what he would say and how he would say it. He would tell Alley that he had no hard feelings and harbored no ill will, but he didn't feel comfortable with the changes Alley had made in the XinoniX cultural fabric and, more important, he'd been frustrated to see their success evaporate before his eyes. He would tell Alley that he was going to work for Cat Cassidy in a very different industry, so he shouldn't be concerned about competition or anything of the sort. He would say that he hoped he was wrong about the future of XinoniX, that he really hoped they would turn things around. He would say that, despite all of this, he wished Alley well. And that he'd be happy to help smooth his departure and take whatever time would be necessary to do so in the least disruptive way. He had planned his little speech word for word and rolled it over in his mind hundreds of times. But he never got the chance to deliver it.

Within fifteen minutes of hitting "send" on his email, Jan from HR, accompanied by someone from security, arrived at Jimmy's desk, watched him gather his belongings, and escorted him to the sidewalk outside the building.

And so ended the storied XinoniX career of young Jimmy Sun.

CHAPTER 28

Since the day that Jimmy jetted from XinoniX and landed at YSC, I continued to hear great things about him from Cat. She was so taken with him, in fact, that she considered him to be chief of staff material and was personally mentoring him with that in mind for his next career step.

I no longer had any direct contact with anyone at XinoniX, so all I knew was what I heard through the grapevine or read in the business press. And none of it was good.

The layoffs that Jimmy predicted had unfortunately come to pass. But the cuts were much deeper and broader than anyone expected. The latest word was that they were closing the headquarters in Sorrento Valley and relocating the small, skeletal staff of survivors to an office park in Poway, near where I lived.

In a momentary fit of nostalgic melancholy, I thought back to the first time I'd visited that XinoniX building some twenty-five years before, when Janice was the senior VP of marketing and Bob Jeffers was the newly appointed, micromanaging CEO who'd taken over the helm when the founder, Teddy Garrison, had mysteriously stepped aside. I thought about Jeffers, who, as you've already heard, dramatically changed from his autocratic ways. And I remembered with pride how he and Janice had become the core of a great team that brought the company into its golden years.

The rest, as they say, is history. And, sadly, that's all it was now—history.

The most notable person to have been jettisoned in the recent XinoniX maelstrom was one Alastair Langstrom. To be more accurate, I'd read that he'd "resigned to pursue other opportunities," but we all know what that really means.

From a few people whom Alley and I knew in common, I learned that he had left California and relocated to Minnesota. At first that sounded like an odd move, but then I remembered that he was very close with his sister and her family, who all lived in the Minneapolis–St. Paul area. I wondered if he went home to lick his wounds in the safe company of people he loved and trusted. But that assumed that he had any wounds to lick. I was curious what, if anything, he'd learned from his failed experience as a CEO, or if he'd even considered it a failure at all.

A quick Google search on my desktop computer revealed that Alley had already taken a position as chief marketing officer for a Minneapolis-based, family-owned shoe company. At first blush, going from CEO down to CMO looked to me like a setback, career-wise. And going from the high-tech world to shoes, of all things? How would that feel for him? But on closer examination, I saw that the company had a long history, a strong brand, and a global presence, which meant that Alley's responsibilities could potentially be greater and more far-reaching than any of the mid-sized tech companies where he'd had C-suite roles so far—including CEO of XinoniX.

Oh boy, I thought.

And, for the time being, I let it go at that.

My gloomy pondering was happily interrupted by an email message inviting me to speak at an upcoming conference in San Jose.

Far be it from me to turn down a speaking gig, and, given the location of this one, it held the promise of an additional bonus. It had been too long since I'd seen Jim and Barry, so I excitedly texted the guys to tell them I'd be in their neighborhood and suggested that we get together for a late lunch catch-up at a place of their choosing.

And when they picked the Chat Bar and Grill in Menlo Park, I literally laughed out loud.

"LOL and OMG," I texted them in our group chat. "That's where I first interviewed Alley."

"We know," Barry texted back.

CHAPTER 29

When I walked into the Chat, as the locals called it, it brought back the memory of my first, fateful meeting with Alley, which in some ways felt like eons ago. Once again, I noticed the warmth of the place. It wasn't just the temperature; it was the understated comfort that comes from soft light, polished wood, and the quiet hum of conversation. The air carried a faint mix of oak and roasted meats, the kind of scent that always made me want to linger.

To my left, the bar stretched out in dark wood and brushed brass, gleaming under a line of pendant lamps. Several customers leaned on their elbows, half-turned toward the bartender, who, I imagined, knew all their names—and drinks—by heart. The rhythm of the place felt steady and unhurried, which provided a nice contrast to the mostly frenetic lives of the kinds of people who frequented this place. Beyond the bar, clusters of tables were spaced generously apart, set with leather chairs that had some weight to them.

On the far side, a stone fireplace anchored the room, and at a square table just to the left of it, I saw my old friends and mentors waving me over to join them.

They stood to greet me and gave me warm, welcoming hugs before we sat down and settled in for what would prove to be more than a quick reunion. Jim sipped on his usual Arnold Palmer and Barry his Diet Pepsi. Waiting for me in my place was a bottle of sparkling water and a glass of ice with a wedge of lime.

"We ordered for you," smiled Barry as I twisted open the bottle.

"We know your drink," said Jim.

"You should have been bartenders," I said, gesturing toward the guy working the bar behind me.

We exchanged a few pleasantries and had some laughs at each other's expense, as old friends often do when they're catching up. And then Jim's face turned serious, and I got the impression he was feeling a little nervous, or hesitant to say something.

Barry jumped in. "We have something to tell you," he said.

"We would have talked to you sooner, but we promised we wouldn't," said Jim.

"Promised who?" I asked, as I took a swig of my drink. I was more curious than anything else.

"Alley," they said, almost in unison.

This would have been a great moment for me to execute a spit take, as they call it in comedy. But I managed to swallow my mouthful of Pellegrino.

"Say what?" I said. "When . . . how?" I had so many profound questions.

"Okay," Jim said. "Here's what happened. A little while ago, Alley called Barry at his office at Santa Clara." His voice trailed off when he noticed his partner's raised eyebrows. "Oh, right. Sorry. You tell him, Barry."

"So, a little while ago, Alley called me at my office at Santa Clara," Barry repeated with a wry smile. "He said that he knew of Jim's and my work, he'd heard that our 'books were great,' and he was wanting to engage us for some advice. He also knew of our connection with you, so he wanted assurances that we wouldn't involve you in our conversations or even tell you that we were talking."

"Until such time as he would give us permission to do so," Jim interjected.

"Which he has since done," said Barry.

"Okay," I said, fidgeting in my seat. "And? So? What happened?" The suspense was killing me, as the saying goes.

"First of all, let me be clear," Barry continued. "I told Alley that Jim and I had been hearing about him from you. And that we'd met Janice, who had also shared with us her experience and frustration. I wanted him to know that we realized any preconceived notions we had of him were entirely through the filter of your and Janice's perception."

"Good disclaimer," I said. "And he was okay with that?"

"More than okay," said Barry. "He said he liked the idea of having someone else's points of view about his leadership."

I raised my eyebrows—the skeptical, universal sign for *yeah, riiiiiight.*

"All he asked was that we would be as objective as humanly possible in helping him to map out and plan for his next career move."

"At the shoe company?" I asked.

"Yes," said Jim. "At the shoe company." He sounded surprised I'd known about that.

"Google," I said, giving a one-word answer to Jim's unasked question.

"So anyway," Barry said, cutting to the chase, "I was intrigued. I spoke with Jim, and we agreed to meet with Alley, have a conversation, and see what happens."

"We felt it would be worth it if we could help him learn from his XinoniX experience and show up as a better, more credible leader in his new position," added Jim.

"And that's what Alley said he wanted? To be a 'better, more credible leader'?" I asked, incredulous. "That sounds, um . . . out of character, to me."

"Specifically," Barry clarified, "he said he wanted to 'hit the ground running.'"

"Ah, well," I said with a forced, impish smile. "If the shoe fits . . ."

They winced and chortled at my bad dad joke and told me that Alley had flown up to see them, and they ended up spending an entire day together. First, Alley gave them a high-level account of his time at XinoniX, and even though he was clearly disappointed by the final outcome, he took virtually no responsibility for the disaster and cast the blame at everyone else—Janice (she was *irresponsible*), Jimmy (*little backstabber*, he'd called him), the culture (*too soft and squishy*), the board (*clueless*), and even the physical office space (*excessive and ludicrously expensive*).

Ultimately, Alley told them, he had seen the writing on the wall and resigned before said "clueless" board had a chance to fire him.

"Wow," I said, after hearing their recap of Alley's story. "I'm not surprised, but it's still disappointing. I'd like to think he'd have taken at least some measure of accountability."

"Well," said Jim, "we weren't done yet. Now it was our turn to chime in."

"So we started with a question," Barry said as he waved to catch our server's attention. "What did you learn from your time at XinoniX? And what, in retrospect, might you have done differently?"

"Did he have an answer?" I asked.

"He said that maybe he could have listened more."

"That's it?"

"Well, it was a start," Jim chuckled. "But we clearly had a few things to add for his consideration."

Late afternoon was tipping into evening, so we switched our drinks to something more suitable for the time of day. Jim and I ordered a couple of glasses of pinot, and Barry a Bombay Sapphire and tonic. Not that those details were particularly important, but it signaled to me that we weren't even close to wrapping things up.

Well, if that's the case . . . I thought.

So I ordered up a charcuterie board of smoked meats, cheeses, and sourdough wedges to keep our fires burning and blood sugars on an even keel.

Their next step with Alley, they continued, was to give him a tutorial, of sorts. A lesson that Alley could use in his next gig, if he so desired: a kind of Kouzes and Posner short course on the elements of credibility. A checklist, if you will, that would wrap up Alley's recommended leadership priorities in a neat little package that—in my humble though educated opinion—he would be a total freaking clodpole to ignore.

Given all that I knew about the man in question, I was eager to know the details. So I asked them to lay out the items for me just as they had for Alley.

"Sure," said Jim. "We'd be happy to."

"Hey!" exclaimed Barry. "I have an idea. Why don't we role-play this?"

"What do you mean?" I asked.

"You be Alley, and we'll be . . . well, us."

"I love it," Jim said, smiling at me. "You do your best to represent Alley's point of view, and we'll—as you say—lay it out for you just as we did for him."

"Well, I . . ."

"Ready, *Alley?*" Jim began, turning in his chair to face me directly.

I guess we're doing this, I thought.

And, digging deep into my frustrated ambitions of one day becoming an Oscar-winning method actor, I allowed myself to inhabit the soul and psyche of my old pal Alastair.

CHAPTER 30

"Number one," Jim began. "*Leadership is a relationship*. It's a relationship between those who aspire to lead and those who choose to follow. So, Alley, when you assume your new role as chief marketing officer in a company where you don't know anyone, the first thing you need to do is spend time with the people who'll be reporting to you and learn as much about them and their jobs as you can. You need to cultivate and build relationships because, ultimately, you want them to *choose* to follow you, not simply to follow your orders because you're the boss. If all they do is follow orders, they'll never go above and beyond with their own initiative, imagination, and ingenuity. And the top four characteristics people look for in a leader they would *willingly* follow are that that person is honest, competent, inspiring, and forward-looking. That's what they'll want to experience in their relationships with you. And, with the exception of forward-looking—aka vision—those characteristics add up to one word: *credibility*.

"Which leads us to number two: *Credibility is the foundation of leadership*. If you don't believe in the messenger, you won't believe the message. Without credibility, you have nothing. Every leadership book you ever read, every course you ever take, every coaching session—like this one, for example—that you ever participate in will be moot if you're not seen as credible by your constituents. This simple but critical truth has come to be known as the *Kouzes-Posner First Law of Leadership*."

"That begs the question of what credibility looks like," Barry tagged in. "The Kouzes-Posner Second Law of Leadership, and number three on the list, is *Do what you say you will do—DWYSYWD*. Think of it as the behavioral definition of credibility. It's the consistency and constancy between your words and your deeds, and it has two core elements: 'Do' and 'Say.' That means that first you're going to need to be clear about what you'll want to *say* to people in your role as CMO. What will you tell them about your expectations, priorities, goals, and commitments? You'll need that clarity in order for you to consistently follow through and put those words into actions, which is the *do* element of DWYSYWD.

"And this doesn't require perfection, either. Our research shows that leaders who are perceived by their direct reports as 'almost always' following through on their promises and commitments are trusted nearly ninety times more than those who are seen as only 'sometimes' (or less) doing what they said they would do."

"Okay," I said, assuming my assigned persona. "Let me tell *you* about the first and second laws of Alley. Number one: I'm the boss. Number two: I'm the boss. Which means you do what I say you will do."

Hey! This was fun.

"How well did that work for you at XinoniX, *Alley*?" Jim said, taking the bait and stepping out of character a bit.

"There's only so much you can do when you're surrounded by apathy and incompetence," I said, channeling the most cartoonish version of Alley I could conjure in the moment. This was great therapy.

"Time out! Cut!" laughed Barry, stepping in to direct the scene. "To be clear, Alley was actually quite receptive to what we shared with him. And Jim and I had decided to focus him on the future instead of the past, so we didn't spend a lot of time rehashing or debriefing his XinoniX tenure."

"Well, that's no fun," I said.

"How about this," Barry smiled. "We'll still talk to you as if you're Alley, but . . ."

"But I keep my mouth shut," I said.

"No, keep pushing back as you think Alley would. But just know that he was really quite open to our ideas and suggestions, so you don't have to go overboard with the cynicism and deflection stuff."

"Okay . . . good note, Mr. Director," I said, assembling a few pieces of the food that had just arrived. "I'm ready."

"Moving on," said Jim as I took a bite. "Fourth on our list is the reality that *values drive commitment*. The place for you to begin earning and sustaining personal credibility with others is actually inside yourself. You'll need to explore your inner territory to a degree that you may not have ever done before. Who are you, Alley? What do you believe in? What do you stand for? In other words, what are the values that should guide your decisions and actions? The clearer you are on that, the stronger your center of gravity will be when external events get turbulent and chaotic, which they will surely do, and you will be better able to sustain your commitment in good times and bad."

"Okay," I said, jumping back into my Alley role. "I think I'm already pretty clear on what I value. I value performance. I value results. I value progress. I value . . ." my voice trailed off as I tried think of what else to say. "Well, I'm sure there's a lot more, but I need to think about it."

"Yes!" exclaimed Jim. "That's the point: You need to think about it."

"I get it," I said. "But you said that *values drive commitment*, right? But whose commitment? Mine or theirs?"

"Yes," said Jim. "Both."

"In fact," Barry jumped in. "Research shows that being clear about your own leadership philosophy makes you eight times more effective in the eyes of your direct reports. And guess what, Alley?"

Given my new stage direction, I didn't know how much dialogue I should contribute in answer to that, so I opted for the terse approach.

"Um, what?" I replied.

"Everyone else has values, too," Jim responded. "And their values are just as important to them as yours are to you. So, you'll need to *affirm shared values*."

"Which would be number five, if I'm counting correctly," I said.

"Yes, you are," said Barry. "As a leader, you can't assume that just because you're clear about and believe in your own values and beliefs, others share those values with you and agree that they should guide organizational and team decisions and actions. Remember, leadership is a relationship, and strong relationships are built on mutual understanding. So that means you'll need to take the time to discover what other people's values are."

"How am I supposed to do that?" I asked, incredulous, as I imagined Alley would be.

"You ask them," said Jim with a shrug. "Obvious, right? And then you listen—I mean, really listen—to their answers."

I didn't say anything; instead, I executed my very best Alley eyeroll.

"Alley," Barry said to me. "You just told us that you value performance, right?"

"I did say that, yes. Performance is key. So?"

"So," Barry continued. "A little more research for you: There's a 40% increase in overall performance for those leaders who have mastered the practice of listening and responding with empathy. By doing so, you're not only learning about what's important to them, but you're also demonstrating that you care about what they think and that you value who they are. Direct reports feel valued by their organizations in direct proportion to how they feel listened to and understood by their leaders. And the more valued they feel, the better they perform.

"And in those conversations, you'll discover where your and everyone else's values overlap and align—and, rest assured, there will be lots of areas of alignment. Then your responsibility will be to demonstrate how your team's areas of alignment support and contribute to the published, long-standing values of the company's vision, mission, and values. Honor them. Talk about them. And let them guide your decisions. And you'll see the results. Simply put, shared values make a difference in people's commitment, productivity, and overall feelings of efficacy and importance. Conversely, if people feel that they can't be true to themselves while following the stated values of the whole group, they won't be highly committed. And they are more likely to leave when times get tough."

"Which brings us to number six," said Jim, continuing their back-and-forth cadence. "*Leaders set the example*. Credible leaders know that it's through their visible actions that their true commitment is demonstrated. So what does that mean for you, Alley? You go first. Show everyone how important your shared values are by spending some of your precious time every day to create systems and processes that support those shared values. Hold yourself accountable to the same—or higher—standards as everyone else. And go out of your way to recognize others for their service to shared values. Don't just DWYSYWD. You also need to DWWSWWD—Do What We Say We Will Do. You be the walking, talking, living, breathing example of what it means to live by the values that we all say are important."

"Number seven was best said by our mutual friend, Steve Farber," Jim continued.

"Well, I don't know about *friend*," I said, as Alley about myself. This was getting confusing. "But he is a really, really, really, really, really smart guy."

"That's way too many *reallys*," said Barry. "But, still . . . Farber calls it being a *Greater Than Yourself*, or GTY, mentor to others. He says that 'the truly great leaders in life become so because they cause others to be greater than themselves.' If all you do is act out of self-interest—or if others perceive that's what you're doing—you erode the bond that connects people to you and to your shared values. But if you lead in service of others, if you invest in their path, if you strive to increase their capacity and expand their competence and influence so that they can go on to surpass even your own success, not only will they see you as eminently credible, they'll be deeply grateful for the impact you've had on their lives. And you can do that without sacrificing one iota of your own accomplishments. You will in fact greatly expand yourself in the process. Your personal influence and reputation will grow, and you will become known as the leader who creates superstars. That's how you'll be remembered. That will be your legacy. And you will create such goodwill that any time you need help solving a problem or meeting a challenge, or whenever you need to recruit talent for your team or company, people will come running. So, as you're building the relationships with your new team, be on the lookout for ways you can lift other people up to heights greater than they've achieved in their careers before you came along."

"Wow," I said, breaking character and choking up a bit. "I'm on your list. I don't know what to say about that. I'm honored."

I shook it off and continued as some approximation of Alley.

"So, is that it?"

"Nope," said Jim. "There's one more. And for you especially, Alley, it's a big one: *You can't do it alone.* We implore you to remember that no one ever—*ever*—makes extraordinary things happen all by themselves, especially in organizational settings. Excellence is always a team effort, my friend."

"One more factual tidbit," said Professor Barry. "Leaders who very frequently cultivate cooperative relationships with their colleagues are overwhelmingly regarded as the finest leaders people have worked with. In fact, over 90% of direct reports say so."

"So," concluded Jim, "the more you develop the capacity of others—yes, through a GTY approach—but also by taking every opportunity to promote learning, share information, strengthen others, and foster ownership across the board, the greater the chance will be that your new adventure in the C-suite will be your best one yet."

"That was great," I said, raising my glass in a toast to wrap up our little dramatic reenactment. "I think Alley may have set a record at XinoniX by doing the opposite of almost every one of those elements. I wish you guys could have been talking in his ear the whole time he was there. Do you think you reached him?"

Jim and Barry glanced at each other and shrugged.

"That'll be for the folks at the shoe company to answer," said Jim.

"Instead," said Barry. "How about we put our attention where we have an opportunity to make a big difference for someone else?"

"Sure," I said. "Like where?"

"Well," said Jim. "Like with Janice and her new venture."

I hadn't known that she was still in touch with them, so I was surprised that they knew about it.

"Well, yeah," I said. "That would be great. How much have you heard?"

"Only everything," smiled Barry.

CHAPTER 31

It was the opening day celebration of the newly rechristened WG Maritime Shipping Masters, and I could feel the energy in the air as I pulled into the company's lot. It was, of course, seventy-two degrees and sunny in San Diego, which made this a perfect day for an outdoor fete.

A massive grill was fired up and churning out fresh barbeque for what looked like a couple hundred Maritime employees and their friends and families, who were all milling around the large, open grassy area next to the building.

On the edge of the grass, a stage platform was set with a PA system, mic stands, amplifiers, a keyboard, and a drum kit, which meant, of course, that there'd be a live band. My heart jumped in anticipation of who that might be.

I milled through the crowd, said hello, shook hands, and exchanged hugs with the folks I'd met during my previous visit and introduced myself to their guests.

Across the way, I saw Janice talking and laughing with a small gaggle of people. Standing next to her was someone who, from this angle, looked a lot like Jimmy Sun.

Huh, I thought, *that's a nice surprise. I wonder what he's doing here.*

"Over here!" someone shouted to me.

I turned and found myself looking directly into a camera lens.

"Gotcha!" the photographer exclaimed as he rapid-fired the shutter. Surprised, I gave him a delighted high-five.

"Simon! What are you doing here?" That seemed like it was going to be the question of the day.

"I heard there was a special party going on, and I didn't want to miss it," said Simon. "And I had a feeling it's going to turn out to be a historic day for our friend Janice. So here I am to immortalize the festivities!"

In the distance over Simon's shoulder, Janice was standing by the stage, waving her arms to catch my attention and summoning me over to her. With an affectionately snarky comment about *Her Majesty's beckoning*, I took my leave of the Bolt's alter ego and sauntered over to the woman of the hour.

I was truly excited for her. She'd been through quite the dramatic journey lately, and I was proud of her for how she'd proven herself to herself. As I approached, I felt myself beaming ear to ear with a smile that felt like it was emanating directly from my heart.

"Well, you look happy," Janice laughed when she saw me.

"I am," I said. "For you, my friend."

Smiling, she took my arm and walked me around to the back of the stage, which was a kind of makeshift green room hidden in the shadow of a framed curtain backdrop.

"Okay!" Janice shouted. "Now the gang's all here!"

And what a gang it was. I felt like I was joining in on a reunion of some of my most treasured friends and associates. Seeing them all together, in this moment, literally made my face hurt from a smile that couldn't have gotten any bigger without some serious facial reconstruction. I'd assumed that they were all here to celebrate Janice's new venture. But it turned out to be much more than that.

Cat Cassidy, Jimmy Sun, Bob Jeffers, Jim Kouzes, Barry Posner, and Janice. All together. In one place. It was borderline surreal, but in the most wonderful way. My first thought was that Janice was the common denominator among them, so it made sense that she'd invited them all.

"Farber," said Janice, taking my hand in hers. "You know how much I've valued your friendship, advice, and counsel over the years, right?"

"Um . . . yes?" I found myself bewildered by her suddenly dramatic tone. What was going on here?

"So I really, really hope that you'll take this as a tribute to your influence and impact."

"Um . . ." I was repeating myself. "Take what?"

"You realize," she continued, "that you facilitated the coming together of the three worlds represented in this group of extraordinary people: the world of XinoniX compadres, the world of Cat Cassidy, and the world of Kouzes and Posner. Without your care and concern for me, this constellation would likely never have formed."

I looked at the affirming smiles on their faces.

"Well, sure. Now that you mention it. I guess that's true."

"Well," she said. "I just want to tell you that we've been conspiring a little behind your back. And now it's time to come clean."

"Geez," I said, bristling a little at the suspense. "You're killing me here. Come clean about what?"

"This exceptional collection of human beings is now officially on my team," Janice said with a sweeping gesture.

"Really? How so?"

"Yes. Really! First of all, allow me to introduce you to my new chief of staff: Mr. Jimmy Sun."

Jimmy took a deep, ceremonial bow.

"Wow!" I exclaimed. "That's fantastic news! And Cat's good with that?"

"Of course," Cat responded. "As board chair of WG Maritime Shipping Masters, I highly endorse it," she said, feigning a pompous, affected tone.

"Next," Janice continued. "May I present the first two members of our advisory board, the DWYSYWD duo themselves, Messrs. James M. Kouzes and Barry Z. Posner."

"Hi, how are ya?" said Jim extending his hand.

"Nice to meet you," said Barry, following suit by playing along.

"Yeah. I've heard of you guys," I snorted. "How long have you two known about this?"

"We've been talking for quite a while," Janice answered for them. "Remember that day on the rooftop when you and Bob challenged me to write a Credo Memo?"

I looked over at Jeffers. "Of course. What about it?"

"Well, I wanted to follow through. But I really struggled with it, as you know. So, on my retreat to Costa Rica, I reached out to Jim and Barry for help. And, over many a Zoom call, they graciously coached me through it. And in the process, we became good friends. So I asked them to throw in with me as charter advisory board members."

"Didja, now?" I laughed, finding myself inexplicably amused at all the secrecy. "And nobody chose to tell me about it?"

"Well, we didn't choose to *not* tell you," said Jim.

"Actually, I chose to not tell you," Janice admitted, taking my hand. "I felt that you had already done so much for me by bringing these amazing people into my circle. And I guess I just wanted to honor that gift by proving to you that I could live up to your faith in me and my abilities . . . without calling you every ten minutes."

"You had nothing to prove to me, Janice." I gave her a big bear hug.

"So what's Bob's role in all this?" I said, gesturing to him. "You coming out of retirement, or what?"

"Oh, hell no," he laughed. "I'll be standing by as a resource, of course, but today I'm just here to applaud and provide a little merriment . . . and ammunition."

He pointed to a large tub filled to overflowing with Nerf balls.

I thought back to the pelting I'd received on my visit to the company and chuckled at the memory.

"Way to honor and promote their new tradition, Bob," I said. "That's very cool."

And then I noticed an unexpected feeling of sadness, with maybe a little pinch of jealousy, burbling inside my chest. On the one hand, I was elated at this news. But on the other, I'm reluctant to admit, I had one nagging, overriding question on my mind in that moment: *What about me?*

"So where do I fit in to all this, Janice?" I asked, trying to sound like I'd be fine with any answer.

"Well, I'd love for you to be on the advisory board, too, if you're willing."

"Well, of course," I exclaimed, sounding more relieved than I'd intended. "I'd be honored."

"And I'd like for you to jump back in as my main coach and confidant, if you'd be willing."

"Well, of course," I said, repeating myself yet again.

"But even better than all that, Farber, you get to do something really cool . . ." Janice raised her eyebrows, mischievously.

"Yes?"

"You get to write about it."

CHAPTER 32

Cat and the band wound up their smoking version of Bonnie Raitt's hit "Thing Called Love," which had drawn the partying crowd bopping and dancing up close to the stage.

As the cheering subsided, Cat stepped up to the microphone, tapped it a couple of times, and asked for everyone's attention.

"Ladies and gentlemen," she shouted. "May I introduce to you the one, the only, the legend herself, your CEO of Maritime Shipping Masters . . . Janice Everson!"

And, of course, the crowd went bananas.

Janice approached the front of the stage and pulled a piece of paper from the back pocket of her jeans.

Jim, Barry, and I were standing off to the side with Bob Jeffers and Jimmy Sun. Barry gave me a nudge as Janice unfolded the page and prepared to speak.

"Watch this," he said.

"My friends," Janice began. "I've been thinking a lot about our new company. I've been thinking about the great things we're going to do together. And I've been thinking about you. Your dreams. Your hopes. Your aspirations for the future.

"But most of all, I've been thinking about us. About what we can achieve together. Because as my friends Jim Kouzes and Barry Posner often say, *you can't do it alone*. I can't do it. And you can't do it.

"But *we* can."

"Preach!" someone shouted from the back of the crowd, and everyone responded with raucous cheering, whooping, and hollering. As the jubilant noise settled down, Janice continued.

"I also understand that even though we're all in this together, as the leader in this venture, my job is to be the best person that I can possibly be. My job is to set our highest standards and hold myself accountable for personally living up to them. You deserve nothing less than my very best."

"Here comes her Credo Memo," Jim whispered to me. "She's put a lot of work into this."

"Therefore, my dear colleagues," said Janice. "I'd like to share with you the principles, the values, the beliefs that I hold dear. As your friend, your colleague, and your CEO, I will strive to live up to these every day, in everything I do, in every action I take, in all the decisions I make and in the ones that we make together.

"This is my radical promise to you . . ."

Janice Everson looked out at the upturned faces of her team, took a deep breath, and began.

Putting Promise into Practice

A Field Guide for Action

The Radical Promise

> I embrace the reality that doing what you say you will do is not just important, it is imperative. Therefore, I make a Radical Promise to hold myself 100% accountable to my own words. DWYSYWD is not a platitude.
>
> It's not a truism. It's a deep, soul-based commitment to the authentic core of who I am.
>
> All of this requires a significantly heightened sense of self-awareness, where I truly think before I speak.
>
> And once I speak, I know that it is not acceptable to retract.

> Having said that, I acknowledge that I am not perfect—no one is.
>
> I recognize that this is an impossible standard to live up to in an absolute and literal sense.
>
> But it is a truly significant, monumental aspiration to have for myself, because in the striving to live up to it, I create a much higher rate of consistency between my words and my actions.
>
> And that's all I can ask of myself as a fallible human being.
>
> Once I have established that standard for myself, it gives me the credibility to ask the same of others—which I fully intend to do.

Dear Reader:

We left our telling of Janice's story as she was about to share her Credo Memo with the members of her new company. Imagine you were in Janice's place. What would you do to prepare for this moment? How do you build a solid foundation so that your constituents (the people you need to influence, whether they're your neighbors, friends, colleagues, direct reports, or manager) will believe in you and know you will DWYSYWD? Where do you begin? How do you get started?

To these questions and probably many others that may have come up in your reading of *The Radical Promise,* we'd like to offer a framework to help guide you along the path to becoming an even more credible leader. Even if you've already taken some of these actions that follow, consider them again and think about other new ideas that can work for you. You can't take your credibility for granted; you have to earn it every day.

Keeping your promises, as you'll note in this section, ultimately depends on the degree to which you Discover Yourself, Appreciate Others, Affirm Shared Values, Set the Example, and Develop Capacity. You can see examples of all of these throughout this leadership parable—from the importance of discovering your own values, like Janice was forced to after her departure from XinoniX, to the way that Alley failed to appreciate the concerns of those around him, and in his lack of alignment with shared values, in the example set by Cat and eventually Janice, and how the new company set up everyone for success.

Discover Yourself

> DWYSYWD is not a platitude.
>
> It's not a truism. It's a deep, soul-based commitment to the authentic core of who I am.
>
> All of this requires a significantly heightened sense of self-awareness, where I truly think before I speak.

Constituents rightfully expect their leaders to have the courage of their convictions. They expect them to stand up for their beliefs. But if leaders are not clear about what they believe in, they are likely to change their positions with every fad or opinion poll. Without core beliefs and with only shifting positions, would-be leaders will be judged as inconsistent and will be derided for being "political" in their behavior. The first signpost on the credibility development journey reads, *Know Thyself.*

Begin enhancing credibility by exploring your inner territory. Reflect on such questions as: Who are you? What do you believe in? What makes you someone others would *willingly* follow? Use the following exercises to help you narrow in on the values that are most essential for you. Those values represent your convictions.

Clarify Your Values

Being credible as a leader to others begins by first clarifying your own values, the standards by which you choose to live your life. Values guide how you feel, what you say, what you think, how you make choices, and how you act.

Here's a question to stimulate your thinking about your deeply held beliefs: "What are the values—the enduring beliefs—that guide my daily decisions, commitments, and actions?" There are hundreds of words in the English language that can be used to identify your values, providing clarity and allowing for subtle nuances. It is incumbent on you to give the value word definition and meaning. Table 1 has a list of sixty-one value words (arranged in alphabetical order) to get your thinking started.

Table 1 My Most Important Values

Achievement	Flexibility	Productivity
Autonomy	Freedom	Quality
Beauty	Friendship	Recognition
Caring	Fun	Respect
Challenge	Growth	Responsibility

Communication	Happiness	Risk-taking
Competence	Harmony	Security
Competition	Health	Service to others
Cooperation	Honesty	Spirituality/Faith
Courage	Hope	Strength
Creativity	Independence	Teamwork
Curiosity	Innovation	Trust
Customer focus	Integrity	Truth
Decisiveness	Intelligence	Uniqueness
Dependability	Justice	Variety
Determination	Learning	Wealth
Discipline	Love	Wisdom
Diversity	Loyalty	________
Effectiveness	Open-mindedness	________
		________
Equality	Order	________
Family	Patience	________
Fairness	Power	________

This is not an exhaustive list, but it includes many of the most frequently mentioned words. Look over this list and circle as many as fifteen (15) that you consider most important in guiding your decisions and actions at work. There are no wrong answers; all of these are important—some more, some less. If you don't find a value on this list that is important to you, then use the lines provided at the end to add the word that best expresses an important value.

To deepen the clarification process, after selecting your words, go back over the value words you circled in Table 1 and write the five (5) that you hold most dear in the space below. See if you can put them in order of priority. Or give them an importance rating from 1 (low) to 10 (high). Or place them on a continuum. Forcing yourself to express preferences helps you see the relative strength of each value.

____

____

____

____

____

It's impossible to live up to every value there is, but it should be quite doable to stay true to a few cherished ones. Having identified these essential values, do what others have done, and post them on the wall, display them on an office mug on your desk, embed them in a screen saver, or write them on a Post-it® note and place it on your keyboard. Keep these "top of mind" so that you remain true to them in your actions (that is, DWYSYWD).

Discover Your Life Themes

Another way you can determine and access your values is to reflect deeply on your past. Your past is prologue. While leaders look ahead to the future, they also look back to their past to discover forces that may propel them forward. When you explore your past, you'll notice recurring themes. For example, a childhood love of reading fiction might translate to a value for empathy and putting yourself in someone else's shoes. Early experiences with scouting may have embedded within you their motto of "always leaving the campsite better than you found it" and help to explain your environmental interests. Or perhaps growing up in your family's small retail store helped you appreciate the importance of customer service and fostered the importance you place on active listening.

In discovering these life themes, you can discern meaning from what might otherwise seem like a random stream of events. People's lives are frequently shaped by reaction to a significant event or personal challenge in early life. Admired elders and historical figures may have served as role models and can be the inspirations for the unifying forces that create meaning in your life.

Discover your life themes by exploring your own past. Begin by considering some of the following questions:

- What books made the biggest impression on me as a child? What values did these books espouse?
- Who are my most admired historical leaders? What values did I learn from studying them?
- What older persons in my early life did I admire? What values did I learn from them?
- What was a significant challenge early in my life? How did I react? What purpose did I find in it? What values did it teach me?

Evaluate Your Values

How can you know if you truly hold a value? Ask yourself these questions about each of the five value words you previously identified:

- Did I freely choose this value? If it's an organizational value, do I freely choose to accept it?

- Have I considered other alternatives to this value and explored them fully?
- Have I considered the alternative consequences of this value?
- Do I truly cherish this value? Is it something I prize? Am I passionate about it?
- Am I willing to publicly affirm that I hold this value?
- Am I willing to act on this value? Repeatedly, over time, in a consistent pattern?

If your answers to all these questions are "Yes," then you're affirming your choices. If you said "No" to any of them, then you must spend some time reexamining the values you've chosen. Recommit or make a change. Janice, for example, "knew" she held the LEAP beliefs, but it wasn't until she was forced to reexamine them that she realized that she wasn't putting them into practice.

Engage in Dialogue

As you articulate the principles you believe are important to live and to work by, others may wonder, "What do they mean by that?" Your search for a response and the resulting dialogue can increase your understanding of yourself and enable others to increase their understanding of you.

Ask a trusted colleague, mentor, friend, or partner to engage in a dialogue about the values you've chosen. Give them a copy of your list of guiding values. Tell them you want them to play the role of a reporter whose only job is to ask you two questions: "What does that word mean to you?" and "Why is that (value) important to you?" Ask them to continue questioning you until they completely understand what you mean by the values you've selected.

Write Your Credo

Once you're clear and satisfied with the essential values you've chosen, write a Credo Memo. This is a powerful way to summarize and communicate to others the values you believe should guide your decisions and actions. One way to get started on your Credo Memo is to imagine the following scenario:

> Your organization has afforded you the chance to take a six-month sabbatical, all expenses paid. You will be going to a beautiful island where the average temperature is about eighty degrees Fahrenheit during the day. The sun shines in a brilliant sky, with a few wisps of clouds. A gentle breeze cools the island down in the evening, and a light rain clears the air. You wake up in the morning to the scents of tropical flowers.
>
> You may not take any work along on this sabbatical. And you will not be permitted to communicate with anyone at your office or plant. Not by letter, phone, email, social media posts, blogs, carrier pigeon, or any other means. Just you, a few good books, some music, and your family or a friend.

> But before you depart, you've been asked to let those with whom you work know what are the principles that you believe should guide their actions in your absence. They need to know the values and beliefs that you think should steer their decision-making and action-taking.
>
> You are permitted no long reports, however. Just a one-page memorandum.
>
> If given this opportunity, what would you write on your one-page Credo Memo?

Take out one piece of paper and draft that memo.

It usually takes about ten to fifteen minutes to write a Credo Memo. This exercise is not a substitute for more in-depth self-discovery, but it provides a useful reference point for articulating your guiding principles. You can take more time to revise and craft your Credo Memo draft in the future, so don't delay now writing down your immediate thoughts.

Appreciate Others

> We had a culture that was rooted in love and appreciation for each other's contributions.

We can't stress this enough: You can't do anything extraordinary all by yourself.

Leadership is a relationship—a relationship between those who aspire to lead and those who choose to follow. The quality of that relationship strongly influences the extent to which others are engaged in their work and performing at their highest levels. Trust is at the heart of that relationship. The more you're trusted by others, the more likely it is that they will willingly follow your advice, requests, decisions, and actions.

Do you trust more the people you know, or the people you don't know? The people you know, right? Okay, there may be people you know well and don't trust at all, but what's true for most people is that they are more likely to trust those whom they know over strangers. It's not the "Hi, how are you?" kind of knowing that engenders trust. It's the kind of knowing where you know something about what they value, what gives their work meaning, what enriches their lives at home, what their hopes and dreams are, what they cherish about their relationships.

It was Janice's lapse in credibility at XinoniX that created the opportunity for Alley to sweep in and undermine her leadership. Even though she was the known quantity, with a past track record of strong leadership, by not showing up credibly as a leader consistently and continually, the mismatch between her words and actions allowed Alley to sway opinions and hearts (at least temporarily).

To earn and sustain credibility, you must get to know those you lead—especially those closest to you. And they must get to know you, which they can't do if you don't know yourself very well in the first place—which we explored in the previous section. You must fully appreciate others to enable the relationship to work. The greater the extent to which you comprehend others' perceptions, concerns, and values, the greater your ability to work together.

Where and how do you begin? Here are a few practical steps you can undertake to help increase your appreciation of those you work with:

Assess Your Understanding of Others

How well do you understand the values and aspirations of those you lead? On a scale of 1 to 5—with 1 being "not at all" and 5 being "completely"—answer the following questions:

To what extent do I truly understand and appreciate . . .

- The values of my direct reports?

1	2	3	4	5
Not at all	A little	Somewhat	To a great extent	Completely

- The values of my manager?

1	2	3	4	5
Not at all	A little	Somewhat	To a great extent	Completely

- The values of my colleagues?

1	2	3	4	5
Not at all	A little	Somewhat	To a great extent	Completely

- The key values of my external partners?

1	2	3	4	5
Not at all	A little	Somewhat	To a great extent	Completely

Having completed this assessment, now take out a sheet of paper and for those you know well, write down the values you believe are most important to them. What are the shared values among them? Where do their values converge and where might they diverge? Identify the intersection with your own values. Are there any serious gaps?

Ask Everyone to Clarify Their Personal Values

For those whose values you don't understand as well as you should, ask them to do the same "Clarify Your Values" activity you did. Then find a time to sit down and engage in the kind of dialogue with them that you had about your values. Whatever you do, don't assume you know their enduring beliefs until they've told you. Make it a conversation. Share the values you hold dear and ask them to do the same.

Play the role of the reporter in this interaction. Ask those two questions: (1) "What does that word mean to you?" and (2) "Why is that (value) important to you?" Make sure, however, that your tone in this exercise is one that communicates that you're seeking to understand and not to judge. It can be awkward to have this conversation with someone you don't know well, and vice versa, and even more intimidating to have a meeting with people you have a significant professional relationship with (like your manager or key clients and suppliers). A genuinely curious tone will help to lower that stress for everyone.

Another approach with your team is to ask each member to write a Credo Memo, as you did. Give them the same instructions and ask them to be prepared to share their memos with the team (and let them know that you will do the same). Identify shared values and themes and consider how they are already reinforced or if they need greater attention. Explore discrepancies, and determine if they are problematic, or possibly simply semantic ("You say potato, I say potahto").

Listen Everywhere and Listen Well

The best thing leaders can do to show others they respect and consider them worthwhile is to reach out, listen, and learn. Feeling heard is itself an affirmation of others' worth. As a leader, don't simply articulate your own philosophy; you must listen to what's important to others. Pay attention. Learn from others. Do whatever it takes to become an even better listener. No matter how good you think you are at listening, make an active plan to improve. Surveys consistently show that "communication" is the number-one skill for success, valued by employers and the general public for everything from job performance and leadership to daily productivity. Listening is key to ensuring understanding, building empathy and rapport, and fostering trust. Listening is also crucial to making your responses relevant and meaningful.

One more thing. Listening can't be from a distance, from reading reports, or from hearing it secondhand. Proximity is the single best predictor of whether two people will talk to one another (and begin a relationship); you must get close to people to communicate effectively. And because, no doubt, many of your constituents cannot come to you, you must go to them, whether in person or virtually.

Learn from Your Colleagues' Stories

Stay attuned to the work and personal stories people share. You can learn a lot by listening to someone tell a story, as well as the kinds of stories they most often tell. Who are the characters in those stories? What are the central themes? What are the morals of those tales? What do the stories tell you about the storyteller? What values and beliefs do they reveal?

Pay attention to your colleagues' "stories" in other ways. For example, notice the mementos, pictures, sayings, photos, and artifacts that are posted in their workspaces. Consider how Janice took the extra step of learning everyone's name, versus having her constituents constantly wear nametags. This is the very beginning of developing a personal relationship, necessitating hearing (asking about and listening to) more about who your colleagues are on a deeper, more personal level. If people are virtual, and all you see is through a small window into their world, ask them to describe the background they choose or something that might be on their desk or walls. Ask them what these things mean to them.

When you hear a story that you think illustrates the kind of values that are important for your team to hear, share your appreciation of their insight and experience. Recognizing another person's story is a powerful way to demonstrate that you're listening and that you appreciate them, and provides another opportunity to illustrate and reinforce core values.

Affirm Shared Values

> After all we've been through together, you and I, we take this moment to remind each other of our mutual love, devotion, and commitment, and we reaffirm that we still mean it.

Shared values form the foundation for building productive and engaging relationships and workplaces. Knowing your values is essential to individual commitment, which is why we started this field guide with this issue. Shared values, however, are the strongest driver of commitment to an organization. Personal credibility means you must Do What You Say You Will Do (DWYSYWD). Leader credibility means you must also Do What *We* Say *We* Will Do (DWWSWWD).

Credible leaders honor individual values—their own and those of others—and they also find common ground on which everyone can stand. They know that shared values make a difference because they give everyone a common perspective and language for collaboration. Leaders show others how their individual values and interests can be satisfied by reaching consensus on a set of values that guides strategic decision-making and execution.

Conflicts inevitably arise in families, teams, and organizations. Shared values provide everyone with an internal compass to help resolve conflicts and disagreements, and to enable everyone to act independently and interdependently, responsibly and publicly. In a credible community, dilemmas are resolved based on principles, not positions. This is especially true in challenging times. When uncertainty is high, shared values provide a framework for aligned actions. Credible leaders passionately affirm these values and speak enthusiastically on behalf of the community.

Remember, you can't achieve greatness all by yourself. Reaching shared values isn't something one person creates and then announces to others. This following exercise is designed to help your team identify shared values and beliefs. These shared values will guide everyone's decisions and actions as you and they DWWSWWD. You can involve all your stakeholders or, if that's too many for a productive session, gather a representative sample of the group.

Convening a Shared Values Summit

1. Invite your entire team—or a group representative of the entire team—to attend a "Shared Values Summit." Before convening the summit, ask everyone on your team to complete the same exercise you did to clarify their personal values, and tell them to bring their completed work product to the summit.
2. Convene the summit and introduce the purpose of this event: *To identify the values that everyone should use to guide decisions and actions.* Tell them they will use their own personal values as a starting point, and they will also get a chance to hear and see what their teammates have chosen as their guiding principles.

3. Distribute individual sheets of Post-it Notes—about ten or so—to each person to use during this exercise. Instruct everyone to record their personal values on these—one value per Post-it. If they have seven values, for example, they'll have seven separate Post-its.
4. While people are recording their personal values on the Post-its, you or a staff member should affix individual sheets of flipchart paper to the room's walls. Eventually, it will look like an art gallery, with individual paintings hung on the walls. In our experience, you'll need around ten to twelve different sheets.
5. Once they have completed recording their values on Post-it Notes, ask them to create a "values affinity diagram"—that is, clusters of values based on their similarity. For instance, someone might have written down "cooperation," and someone else might have said "collaboration." These two principles are similar and can be clustered together.
6. To begin this process, one person posts their values first, with each value on a separate sheet of flipchart paper. Then all participants place each of their Post-its on a sheet with a value similar to one they wrote on their Post-it. If they have five values, they will need to find five values similar to each of their own. If they discover that one or more of their values doesn't fit with any previously posted values, they should start a new values cluster.

7. This process may initially seem chaotic, as everyone roams around looking for where to post their personal values. As more individuals post their values, however, they get accustomed to the task and find it much easier to complete.
8. Once everyone has clustered their values, ask them to walk around the "gallery" and look at what they see. What patterns of values emerge? What do *we* collectively care about? Where are the differences in values? What does this tell us about the enduring beliefs that should guide our decisions and actions?
9. Continue by asking them to name the values (label) around which they have consensus. What are they? Are there some values that seem to stand alone? What are they?
10. Have a conversation about both shared values and areas of difference. What does this exercise reveal about the team's ability to agree on a set of principles that can guide collective action?

Draft a Team Credo

Now it's time to put all of this together into a *Team Credo Memo*—a document that reflects shared values and is based on what people have individually declared as their personal values. Assemble a writing team of your best wordsmiths and ask them to use the work product from the Shared Values Summit to craft a one-page document that expresses the Team's (or Organization's) Credo. Then assemble everyone for a reading of the document. Ask Summit participants to sign their names. Post it prominently in the office, plant, meeting rooms, store, and other areas where people can view it as a frequent reminder of their shared values. Consider starting every meeting with a review of these shared values or asking for someone to share a recent example of how this value was put into practice. About once a year, bring team members together to review how well they followed through on Doing What We Said We Would Do (DWWSWWD). Use the outcomes of these follow-up sessions to consider updates to the Team Credo and actions that will help uphold commitments in the coming year.

Be an Enthusiastic Spokesperson for Shared Values

Once shared values are agreed upon (e.g., Team Credo), you need to speak enthusiastically about them. Let people know that there is a "we" and how "we" are in this together, that what we are doing is important, and that our contributions make a difference. Think of XinoniX colleagues painting "Do what you love in the service of people who love what you do" on a wall as a remembrance of shared values. What energizes people is when their leader speaks with passion about shared beliefs. Your task is to keep people focused by constantly and publicly affirming shared values. When you hear other people speaking about shared values, referring to them in making decisions, you will know that DWWSWWD is happening.

Set the Example

> I embrace the reality that doing what you say you will do is not just important, it is imperative. Therefore, I make a Radical Promise to hold myself 100% accountable to my own words.

If you're going to ask people to follow you into an uncertain future (and if that journey may require challenges and sacrifices), they must believe in you. Before people determine what they think about what you're saying, they decide what they think of you. In turn, what they think of you is mostly predicated on how they have observed your behavior, and on the consistency between your words and your deeds.

This is the "Do" part of *Do What You Say You Will Do*. It's the part where you *practice* what you preach, *walk* the talk, *put* your money where your mouth is, *follow through* on your commitments, and *keep* your promises. People you lead may hear and agree with the words, but they also want to see in your actions that you are as committed as you ask them to be. A judgment of "credible" is handed down when what you say and what you do are consonant. Another essential way that you set an example is how you go about holding others accountable to shared values and standards.

You set the example in obvious and subtle ways. Here are a few categories you can use to reflect on and help increase your awareness of how your actions can influence other people's behavior. Following this list is a *Values in Action* worksheet you can use to take notes on how to apply these ideas.

Spend Your Time and Attention Wisely

How you spend your time is the single clearest indicator to others of what's important to you. Spending time on what you say is important shows that you're putting your resources and energy behind your espoused values. Whatever those values are, they must show up on your daily schedule, meeting agendas, events you attend, people you interact with, and the like if you want people to believe that what you say is in truth what you do.

For example, in the leadership parable, we saw that Janice was spending valuable time on her extracurricular project and failing to meet all her obligations as CEO at XinoniX. This eroded her credibility in the eyes of her constituents. What Janice's story illustrates is that it's not just about meeting the benchmarks of good leadership once; you must show that you take your values seriously by consistently honoring your commitments and the needs of the people who work with and for you.

Use Relevant Language

Try talking about an organization for a day without using the words "employee," "manager," "boss," "supervisor," "subordinate," or "hierarchy." You may find this experiment nearly impossible unless you've been part of organizations that use other terms—words such as "associates," "crew," "cast members," "team members," "partners," or even "constituents."

The organizational lexicon can easily trap people into a particular way of thinking about roles and relationships. Credible leaders understand and are attentive to language because they appreciate the power of words. Words don't just give voice to one's mindset and beliefs; they also evoke images of what people hope to create with others and how they expect people to behave. Consider whether your word choice is inviting collaboration or compliance. For example, when asking everyone to meet deadlines, consider what's more likely to inspire buy-in: "Please provide feedback by EOB today," or "I'd love it if we could get your feedback and thoughts by the end of the day—your perspective is really valuable."

Ask Purposeful Questions

When you ask questions, you send your constituents on mental journeys. Your questions determine the pathway people will follow and the focus of their search for responses. Questions are another tangible indicator of how seriously you take your espoused beliefs by directing attention to the values that warrant focus and energy. Your questions send signals to others about what's important, what you're interested in, and presumably how they should likewise be focused.

If you were to ask, for example, "What have you done today to partner with a colleague on getting the work done?" you're sending a signal about the importance of collaboration. On the other hand, if you were to ask, "What have you done today to reduce the costs of doing business?" you are sending a very different message. Both are legitimate questions, but they indicate very different priorities.

Seek Feedback

How can you know that you're doing what you say (the *behavioral* definition of credibility) if you never ask for feedback about your actions? How can you expect to align your words and actions if you don't know how others perceive them? Asking for feedback gives you a perspective about yourself that only others can see. With this insight, you can make improvements. Feedback is the most valuable source of information for leadership development.

From whom should you ask for feedback? The best sources are those who are most affected by your actions. Yet it's common, and only natural, for some people to feel intimidated by giving feedback directly to their leaders. You might want to use anonymous pulse surveys or engage coaches and consultants to help. It's also important to avoid general requests such as "Do you have any feedback for me?" Instead, for more useful information, ask "How did my actions around the launch of the new process help or hinder your performance?"

You can often make receiving feedback less intimidating by asking for advice instead. For example, "Do you have any advice about how we could have made better use of our time in that meeting?" Remember what we said about the use of language? A simple word change from "feedback" to "advice" can make people more willing to speak up.

Tell Stories

Stories are another way that leaders pass on lessons about shared values and impress upon others the importance of being on the same page. Stories are powerful tools for teaching people what's important and what's not, what works and what doesn't, and what is and what could be.

Through stories, vital lessons are passed along about shared values and the seriousness with which they are taken.

Recall Simon's story about how the man he photographed used a picture on his desk to drum up meaningful conversation and not split himself between work and "real" life. That story was a more powerful illumination of the point—that there's not a separate "work" you and "real" you; that a healthily functioning work organization allows people to bring their real sense of self to work with them—than any lecture could have been.

Reinforce the Behaviors You Want Repeated

How can you embed shared values into the fabric of your team or organization? Measurement systems, for example, are essential for knowing how people are doing, and without that information, efforts to improve performance would be random, at best. We probably don't need to cite much research to underscore how measured performance subsequently affects behavior. You know about keeping score from the games and sports you've played. And it's not just the numbers themselves that are important. It's what you get points for.

In call centers, measuring performance by how long people are on the telephone would probably result in behavior quite different from performance assessed by client satisfaction scores. Analysts scored by their number of clients would likely lead to interpersonal relationships quite different from those assessed by the volume of their book of business. You can also use the symbols and artifacts of workday life as *visible* reminders of a key organizational value. Posters, pictures on walls, items on desks, sayings on coffee mugs, and buttons or pins on lapels can be much more than decorative items.

Confront Critical Incidents

Be mindful that it is not only what you do that matters. You are also evaluated by how consistent your constituents' actions are with the shared values, so you must also hold them accountable. Critical incidents—chance occurrences, particularly at a time of stress and challenge—are a natural part of everyone's life. These are often times when the proverbial "rubber meets the road," providing an opportunity to demonstrate in real time how seriously pronouncements (words) and commitments (promises) are taken, not just in theory. True for yourself, and true for others. Remember that what is reinforced will be what receives the most attention.

Critical incidents offer significant moments of learning about what's valued and what's not, and how to best honor guiding principles. Janice's erosion of leadership was not just about her own credibility but her failure to hold Alley accountable to the LEAP values. Similarly, Ally's disdain for those values quickly eroded the importance of them to everyone in the company.

Values in Action Worksheet

Select one of the team's shared values. Record some ways to align people's actions with that value using the alignment methods in Table 2. Repeat for each shared value.

Table 2 Shared Values

Spend time
Use relevant language
Ask purposeful questions
Seek feedback
Tell stories
Reinforce with formal systems and rewards
Confront critical incidents

Develop a Contractual Attitude

Setting the example by aligning your and your team's actions with shared values—as you did in the previous exercise—is crucial, to be sure. Now let's consider the commitments you make on a day-to-day basis, whether you mean to or not.

Your words matter. Your follow-through matters even more. Consider a one-week experiment in treating your words like promises.

Early in our story, Janice was getting a reputation for dropping the ball and not following through on her own commitments. *Pulling a Janice*, people called it.

Let's make sure that you're not going to get a rep for *pulling a [insert your name here]*.

Cat's idea of *speaking with a contractual attitude* is simple but powerful: "Treat your every utterance as though you've just signed a contract." So, for one week, act as if everything you say is an agreement someone else is counting on. This experiment will help you notice what promises you make—intentionally or not—and how well your actions line up with your words.

1. **Set Up Your Contract Journal**

   Grab a small notebook or device you can keep with you all week. You'll use it to capture any promise you make in real time—no matter how small or casual.
2. **Track Your Overt Promises**

   Whenever you clearly say you'll do something—send an email, make an introduction, meet a deadline—write it down right away. These are your obvious, intentional commitments.
3. **Track Your Implied Promises**

   This is where things get interesting. Pay attention to the offhand comments that someone else might hear as a commitment. Phrases like "We should get together," "I'll take a look," or "Let me think about it" can land as promises, especially when people trust you or depend on you. If it *could* be interpreted as a commitment, write it down.

4. **Score Each Day**

   At the end of each day, review your list. Mark:

   - ✓ for what you followed through on.
   - → for what carries over.
   - ✗ for what you dropped or forgot.

   You're not judging yourself—you're learning.

5. **Look Back at the Week**

   At the end of the seven days, add up what you captured. Then ask yourself:

   - What did I learn about the way I speak?
   - Where did I unintentionally create expectations?
   - How often did my actions match my words?
   - Are there types of commitments I shy away from more than others?
   - Are there people for whom I fulfill more obligations than for others? Why?
   - What surprised me?

This reflection is the real payoff. You'll start to see patterns in your habits, your blind spots, and your strengths. You may also notice how much weight your words carry with others—and how small shifts in awareness can make a big difference in your credibility.

Try it for a week and see what it does for your self-awareness. Consider repeating the practice periodically. Think of it as your own personal credibility audit.

Develop Capacity

> My only job is to unleash their capacity, to give them what they need to shine.

Shared values are essential to sustaining organizational credibility. But no one can do what they say if they don't know how. Without the skills, resources, and support to deliver on promises, team members feel frustrated, discouraged, and demotivated. Credible leaders, therefore, continuously strengthen team members' competence and confidence. They develop people's capacity to act on shared values in ways that enhance the organization's credibility.

Capacity isn't just about skills and resources. It also depends on how people *feel* about themselves. Do they feel valued by their leaders and others in the organization? Do they feel capable and confident to do their jobs? Do they believe they are making a difference?

Also true is that developing the capacity of others demonstrates that you have their best interests at heart. You want them to be the best they can be. Being on the receiving end of this sentiment, and follow-up actions, goes a long way toward establishing trust, a key ingredient for high performance and central to experiencing psychological safety.

We've studied leadership behavior for over forty years, and the evidence is clear. When people work with leaders they admire and respect, they feel better about themselves. Leaders who positively impact others enable them to feel valued and capable of achieving ever-higher levels of performance. Here are several actions you can take to develop capacity:

Perform a Capacity Assessment

Take out a piece of paper and at the top, record one shared value. Below it, answer these questions (and do this for each of the shared values for your team):

Shared Value: ____________________________

To what extent do the people I lead . . .

- Feel a sense of ownership to deliver on this value?
- Feel they have my support to deliver on this value?
- Have the knowledge and skills to deliver on this value?
- Have opportunities to learn how to deliver on this value?
- Feel confident in their abilities to deliver on this value?
- Have the resources they need to deliver on this value?
- Have the decision-making authority to deliver on this value?
- Have the information they need to deliver on this value?

Armed with your responses, what are the actions you need to take to strengthen people's ability to uphold shared values? You may need to ensure everyone understands each of the shared values and how each one is translated into behavior. You might need to provide educational opportunities to help people improve their skills. You might need to increase decision-making authority or better allocate resources so people can deliver. You could also improve information sharing. Whatever these actions are, you now have a plan for building capacity to DWWSWWD.

Make Sure Everyone Feels They Have a Customer

Make certain that whatever people are doing, they have another person or group in their mind that they are serving through their efforts. Without that connection, people will feel alienated from their efforts and unable to be as responsive as they could be. Having a customer (client, buyer, user, partner, patron) also broadens most people's understanding not only of what they do, but also of what the organization does overall. It typically puts each person in direct contact with other parts of the business.

Having customers makes people feel important and significant. One auto mechanic said to us, "I really like it when customers come back and ask for me personally. They say they really liked how I fixed their car and want me to work on it again. That makes me feel great. Proud. I really want to make sure they keep asking for me." Would everyone on your team share this sentiment?

Celebrate Together

Every organizational celebration can serve a dual purpose. One is to offer social support, which makes people happier, healthier, and more productive. The other is to honor an individual, group, or entire organization for upholding a cherished value. People often mark significant historical dates with fireworks, food, drink, and fun. These same celebrations also often recognize cherished values, such as freedom and independence. Organizational celebrations can serve the same purpose. They create opportunities to remind people of the fundamental principles they should honor. They also reinforce how essential it is to ensure that everyone involved has the capacity to live the values cherished.

The opening day celebration of the newly rechristened WG Maritime Shipping Masters is an example of the power of community celebrations. With the nerf balls, massive grill churning out barbeque, musical performance, and Janice's Radical Promise moment, it created an energy that enveloped everyone. It was designed to bring people together, and it did just that. It was also an opportunity to reinforce values and demonstrate to the team how the CEO intended to DWWSWWD.

Encourage Everyone to Recognize Others

When someone has made a meaningful contribution, put a shared value into practice, gone above and beyond their job, or the like, make it easy to let them know that they are appreciated. Set the example yourself (go first) and provide ways for others to recognize their colleagues. For example, have note cards printed that say at the top, "I heard something good about you . . ." Leave enough blank space to write personalized notes describing the reason for their recognition. Give each employee a stack to hand out and encourage them to recognize one another.

Make sure to use them yourself. Place a bulletin board in a visible spot where recipients can display their cards. Set aside time at the start of each meeting for "shout-outs" about what someone (or many) has done that made a difference. When you create a culture in which people recognize and honor their coworkers, you increase the likelihood that everyone is looking for opportunities to honor others for following through on their promises and keeping their commitments.

Be a Greater Than Yourself (GTY) Mentor

Your own greatness as a leader (or in just about any other role, for that matter) lies, paradoxically, in your ability to develop others to be Greater Than Yourself (GTY).

Consider this: If you get a reputation for being the one who elevates people, for being the one who gives freely to others at work, and, as a result, for turning out superstar after superstar who go on to reach higher heights than your own, what do you think is going to happen?

Everyone will want to work with you, that's what. And because of that, you'll be able to accomplish anything you set out to do. Anytime you want or need to get anything done—any idea that you want to pursue, any venture—you'll put out the word, and they'll all come running to help. And for good reason: Everyone will know that by the time your project is completed, your idea implemented, your vision realized, they'll all be that much better for having worked with you, because you will have given them far more than they've given you.

And so it goes, over and over again. Give; get more. Give more; get even more. Consider the possibilities and you'll see why, conversely, keeping others down is eminently unproductive.

Being a GTY mentor to everyone in your life is a very tall order, indeed. So we recommend that you start with just one person you can take on as your "GTY Project." This one-at-a-time approach is a way to develop your own capacity to increase the capacity of others, and soon you'll find yourself taking on more and more mentees.

Choosing someone to mentor, guide, develop, and elevate in this very personal way is not a task to take lightly. This is not about adding an item to your to-do list or "fixing" someone who's struggling. Far from it. It's about making a deliberate and thoughtful choice—one that has the potential to change the trajectory of another person's life *and* your own.

You're not looking for a project to "rescue" or someone you feel needs "saving." GTY is not charity work, and it's definitely not about playing the hero. This is about identifying someone who's ready for growth. It's about recognizing potential in someone who just needs a nudge, a bit of guidance, and a belief in their abilities. They don't need to be fully polished or ready-made for greatness—they just need to have the drive, openness, and willingness to embrace their next level.

When you choose your GTY Project, you're essentially making a bet. A bet on them. A bet on their potential. But here's the kicker—you're also betting on yourself. Because the person you choose will push *you* to grow, to give more, to learn more, and to stretch yourself beyond your current boundaries. This is a two-way street. Your decision here isn't just about them—it's about your own growth as a leader and human being.

So whom will you choose for your GTY Project? Take a few minutes to think about the people in your life. Reflect on those around you—whether in your professional world or personal circles. Who stands out? Who is on the cusp of something more, but just needs a bit of support, a little belief, or a fresh perspective?

Remember, this isn't necessarily about someone being in trouble or needing to be fixed. It's about spotting potential. It's about identifying someone who could go *further* with a bit of help, someone who could reach new heights with your guidance and insight. Consider these questions:

- Who has demonstrated potential but seems held back by circumstance or self-doubt?
- Who has the heart and desire to grow but may lack the direction or confidence to make that leap?
- Who in your life could truly benefit from what you have to offer—your skills, your knowledge, your experience, and your time?
- Whom do you believe in? (Because that belief is where it all starts.)

This is about expanding someone, not *fixing* them. It's about amplifying their greatness, not pointing out their flaws. And by doing so, you're expanding yourself, too.

Write down the names of a few people you could consider for your GTY Project:

1. ______________________________
2. ______________________________
3. ______________________________
4. ______________________________
5. ______________________________

Now, narrow it down to one person. Who is your GTY Project going to be? Write that person's name here: __________ ____ and get started.

For Further Reading

While *The Radical Promise* is a leadership parable, there is solid science behind the lessons the characters learn or demonstrate in the story. To learn more about the research and evidence on how exemplary leadership practices positively influence engagement and performance at work, here are a few other books by Kouzes and Posner you should check out:

James M. Kouzes and Barry Z. Posner, *The Leadership Challenge: How to Make Extraordinary Things Happen in Organizations* (7th ed.). Hoboken, NJ: John Wiley & Sons, 2023.

Jim and Barry have been researching Personal Best Leadership Experiences for over forty-five years, and *The Leadership Challenge* is their seminal work on The Five

Practices of Exemplary Leadership® that emerged from that research. Their findings are described in detail in this book and the evidence supporting the impact of The Five Practices is explored through real-life examples, practical application, and empirical evidence.

James M. Kouzes and Barry Z. Posner, *Credibility: How Leaders Gain and Lose It, Why People Demand It.* San Francisco: Jossey-Bass, A Wiley Imprint, 2011.

Credibility is the second book that Jim and Barry published. In it, they explore what people look for and admire in leaders—the primary finding being that *credibility is the foundation of leadership*—and present strong evidence to support that assertion. *The Radical Promise* draws on this research to tell the story of everyday struggles and rewards of leading with a contractual attitude.

Barry Z. Posner, *Bringing the Rigor of Research to the Art of Leadership: Evidence Behind The Five Practices of Exemplary Leadership and the LPI: Leadership Practices Inventory.* The Leadership Challenge, a Wiley Brand, 2025.

If you're a data nerd, like we are, you'll want to study this whitepaper. It provides a comprehensive overview of the development, validation, and impact of The Five Practices of Exemplary Leadership®. Available free online at https://www.leadershipchallenge.com/resources/assets-gated-details/?id=282

To dive further into the principles, characters, and "universe" of *The Radical Promise*, consider exposing yourself to the insights from Steve Farber's previous leadership and business parables:

Steve Farber, *The Radical Leap: A Personal Lesson in Extreme Leadership*. Chicago: Kaplan Publishing, 2004 (current edition published by Perfect Publishing).

Steve's first business parable grew out of a simple but demanding question: What does leadership look like when you refuse to separate who you are from how you lead? The book introduces the LEAP framework—Love, Energy, Audacity, and Proof—and invites readers to consider leadership as a deeply personal commitment rather than a set of techniques. Several characters who appear in *The Radical Promise* are first introduced here, offering a glimpse into their early struggles, convictions, and defining choices. The story lays the groundwork for understanding leadership as an act of passion, courage, and follow-through.

Steve Farber, *The Radical Edge: Stoke Your Business, Amp Your Life, and Change the World*. Chicago: Kaplan Publishing, 2006 (current edition published by Perfect Publishing).

In Steve's second parable, he continues the story of Extreme Leadership through a narrative that challenges leaders to operate at their "radical edge"—the place where personal values, success in business, and global purpose meet. *Edge* explores how leaders can amplify personal joy, prosperity, and positive impact on the world without sacrificing one for the other. Readers encounter several characters who later reappear or are referred to in *The Radical Promise*.

Steve Farber, *Greater Than Yourself: The Ultimate Lesson of True Leadership*. New York: Currency, 2009; revised edition, 2018 (current edition published by Mission Blvd Press and Digital).

Steve wrote his third parable to convey a simple but demanding idea: Leaders become great by making others greater than themselves. Through a story that weaves together mentoring relationships, lived experience, and the three GTY tenets—Expand Yourself, Give Yourself, and Replicate Yourself—the book explores leadership as a deeply human, relational act rather than a position or title and reinforces a central theme across Steve's work: Credibility is built not by position, but by the love of people and making the choice to invest in them. Some characters who appear in *The Radical Promise* are first encountered here, offering insight into the formative mentoring moments that shaped their approach to leadership and responsibility.

Additional books by Jim Kouzes and Barry Posner:

- *Everyday People, Extraordinary Leadership: How to Make a Difference Regardless of Your Title, Role, or Authority* (Wiley, 2021)
- *The Truth about Leadership: The No-Fads, Heart-of-the-Matter Facts You Need to Know* (Jossey-Bass, 2010)
- *The Student Leadership Challenge: Five Practices for Becoming an Exemplary Leader* (Jossey-Bass, 2018)
- *A Leader's Legacy* (Jossey-Bass, 2006)
- *Learning Leadership: The Five Fundamentals of Becoming an Exemplary Leader* (Wiley, 2016)
- *Encouraging the Heart: Igniting Passion and Providing Meaningful Recognition* (Wiley, 2025)

Additional books by Steve Farber:

- *Love Is Just Damn Good Business: Do What You Love in the Service of People Who Love What You Do* (McGraw Hill, 2019)
- *Twisted Business: Lessons from My Life in Rock 'n' Roll,* with Jay Jay French (French Management Enterprises, 2022)

Acknowledgments

The Radical Promise marks a departure from all our previous books. While we each love telling stories, the three of us had never before collaborated on a leadership parable. But, as they say, timing is everything, and when the opportunity arose, we were all in! Participating in this writing adventure has been a great joy, and we are thankful to each other for the learning, creativity, chemistry, and laughs, and for making it happen together! You could say it was a "radical promise" fulfilled.

Writing a fictional parable informed by real events and inspired by actual people requires knowing a lot of smart, interesting folks—which, fortunately, we do. Unsurprisingly, their influence and experience found their way into the story in both subtle and not-so-subtle ways.

Our sincere thanks to Simon Billsberry, Ilana Wisby, and Mitch Luciano for allowing us to explore—and take some poetic license with—their deeply personal leadership journeys, to the great benefit of the authors and, ultimately, our readers.

Steve Dealph, Chris Groscurth, Cesar Enciso, Burton Goldfield, Rainey Foster, Maurice Thibodeau, Dan Casetta, Bill Courtright, and Adam Markel reviewed and offered feedback on very early drafts and chapters. Their insights gave us greater clarity and confidence as the pages evolved and grew over time.

The book you are holding, reading electronically, or listening to on audio was created through the tireless effort of a dedicated team at John Wiley & Sons. Our gratitude starts with Jeanenne Ray, associate publisher, who saw the potential of a leadership story combining ideas from *The Leadership Challenge* and *Credibility*. Her enthusiasm for *The Radical Promise* was immediate, and she followed through, just as the book's core message teaches. We are deeply grateful to our talented developmental editor, Halley Sutton, who used her experience and insight to ensure the narrative flowed smoothly. She brought out our best with her thoughtful questions, suggestions, and expert editing. Other valued contributors in the Wiley team include Raven Buckler (editorial assistant), Michelle Hacker (senior managing editor), Wendy Lai (cover designer), Amy Handy (copyeditor), Suganya Selvaraj (content refinement specialist), and Michael Frieberg (senior marketing manager).

Whenever we write, we realize we're often taking valuable time away from our wonderful spouses—time spent thinking, conferring, writing, editing, and revising. To them, this process sometimes feels endless. They have been there through the ups and downs, the deadlines and long hours, the frustrations, and the moments of joy. They are always with us, constantly encouraging us, occasionally reminding us to take a break, and regularly sharing brilliant ideas from their own professional experiences that enhance our work. Thank you, Veronica Farber, Tae Moon Kouzes, and Jackie Schmidt-Posner, our Cheer-Leaders-in-Chief, for your love, support, sacrifices, coaching, teaching, and kindness. Without you, we wouldn't be able to make the contributions we aspire to. We love you.

About the Authors

Steve Farber, Jim Kouzes, and Barry Posner have been friends and professional colleagues for over thirty years. Their collaboration began at the Tom Peters Company, where they worked together facilitating workshops around the Five Practices of Exemplary Leadership, as originally described in Jim and Barry's renowned book *The Leadership Challenge*.

Steve eventually founded the Extreme Leadership Institute, where he speaks, consults, and coaches clients in applying the principles you've just read about. Jim and Barry, through many editions of *The Leadership Challenge* and *Credibility* (among other works), have spent five decades researching and working with countless organizations, consistently confirming the timeless veracity of DWYSYWD. Like Steve, they have also spent many years leading organizations. Jim directed executive education centers at two universities for twenty years and was president and then CEO and chairman of the Tom Peters Company for over a dozen. Barry, the Michael J. Accolti Professor of Leadership, in the Leavey School of Business, Santa Clara University, is currently chair of the Management and Entrepreneurship Department and was the dean of the school for twelve years.

Although the story you've just read draws from real people and actual experiences the authors have encountered throughout their careers, the characters are composites drawn from the authors' imaginations and are not intended to represent any specific real individual. Any similarity to actual persons, living or dead, is coincidental. Janice, Alley, Cat, Jimmy, and the others (excepting, of course, the characters of Steve, Jim, and Barry, who, the authors are relieved to know, are very real indeed) are composite characters based on individuals they've known and whose stories reflect circumstances that similarly unfolded.

If you're familiar with the authors' previous work, you'll have recognized many recurring themes, research findings, and case studies woven throughout this parable. These are perspectives on leadership they've developed and refined over decades of practice.

OTHER BOOKS FROM

JAMES M. KOUZES and BARRY Z. POSNER

The Leadership Challenge • ISBN: 978-1-119-73612-7

Encouraging the Heart • ISBN: 978-1-394-30390-8

Everyday People, Extraordinary Leadership • ISBN: 978-1-119-68701-6

The Truth About Leadership • ISBN: 978-0-470-63354-0

WILEY

BRING STEVE FARBER TO YOUR ORGANIZATION OR EVENT

THOUGHT LEADER • BESTSELLING AUTHOR
EXECUTIVE COACH

Steve Farber and his team help leaders transform their organizations through the operationalization of Love, Energy, Audacity, and Proof.

KEYNOTE SPEAKING

Steve delivers high-energy, customized keynotes that move audiences from inspiration to action. His signature presentations—including The Radical Promise: Mastering the Art of Doing What You Say You Will Do, Love Is Just Damn Good Business: Doing What You Love in the Service of People Who Love What You Do, and Greater Than Yourself: The New Mentoring Gold Standard—equip leaders with practical tools to drive engagement, productivity, innovation, and culture change.

EXECUTIVE COACHING & CONSULTING

Through The Extreme Leadership Institute, Steve offers personalized coaching built on the proven LEAP framework. From one-on-one executive coaching to organization-wide culture transformation, he gets deeply personal to expand the power of your influence at every level.

THE EXTREME LEADERSHIP MASTERY CIRCLE

Join a community of leaders committed to mastering Extreme Leadership. The Mastery Circle offers peer-to-peer accountability in an intimate setting, monthly facilitated sessions, and direct access to Steve's coaching—creating continuous momentum toward your boldest goals.

LOVE • ENERGY • AUDACITY • PROOF

Ready for your Radical Promise?

WWW.STEVEFARBER.COM
INFO@STEVEFARBER.COM

THE **EXTREME LEADERSHIP** INSTITUTE